Crystals for Self-Care

Also by the author

Lunar Living
The Lunar Living Journal

Crystals for Self-Care

The ultimate guide to crystal healing

KIRSTY GALLAGHER

First published in Great Britain in 2021 by Yellow Kite
An imprint of Hodder & Stoughton
An Hachette UK company

1

Copyright © Kirsty Gallagher 2021

The right of Kirsty Gallagher to be identified as the Author of the Work has been asserted by her in accordance with the Copyright, Designs and Patents Act 1988.

Illustrations by The Colour Study © Hodder & Stoughton 2021

A CIP catalogue record for this title is available from the British Library

Hardback ISBN 978 1 529 36023 3
eBook ISBN 978 1 529 3602 40

Typeset in Celeste by
Palimpsest Book Production Ltd, Falkirk, Stirlingshire

Printed and bound in Great Britain by Clays Ltd, Elcograf S.p.A.

Hodder & Stoughton policy is to use papers that are natural, renewable and recyclable products and made from wood grown in sustainable forests. The logging and manufacturing processes are expected to conform to the environmental regulations of the country of origin.

Yellow Kite
Hodder & Stoughton Ltd
Carmelite House
50 Victoria Embankment
London EC4Y 0DZ

www.yellowkitebooks.co.uk

For everyone following their True North,
this book is for you.

Contents

Part 2:
Making Crystals a Part of Your Life

Introduction

Welcome! I'm so excited to share the magical world of crystals with you. For those of you who haven't met me yet, my name is Kirsty Gallagher and I'm a moon mentor, soul-alignment coach, yoga and meditation teacher and crystal lover.

I remember getting my first crystal in my early teens, around the same time that my fascination with astrology started. It was a tiger's eye, one of the crystals for my zodiac sign. From then on, I was never far from a crystal and used to carry them around in my pockets or even in my bra!

I started working intentionally with crystals to make changes in my life around 20 years ago, long before they were a trend. I could not believe the support, guidance, clarity, focus, transformation and healing I gained from working with them in a conscious way; for me, it was – and still is – a true act of self-care. I took a course to become a crystal healer in my early

20s and over the years I have undertaken numerous other training courses and workshops to learn more about these magical gifts. And still, to this day, I will gaze at a crystal in total awe that it came from the earth.

Nowadays I work with crystals daily, whether I'm simply wearing one to be in tune with the energies of the crystal or consciously meditating or manifesting with one. Crystals, to me, are loving, loyal friends, offering me invaluable support, and I will often refer to them as such throughout this book to explain the effects and benefits of working with them.

Over the years, I have shared my love of crystals with anyone who will listen. When I was working in a corporate environment, I ensured that almost all my colleagues had one on their desk; and as I moved from that world into teaching yoga, I would gift everyone who came to my workshops a crystal to amplify the work we were doing together.

In *Crystals for Self-Care* I want to share what I have learned over the years with *you*, so that you, too, can feel supported by crystals in the same way I do. As with all my work, I want to make the topic of crystals accessible and relatable – to strip away the confusion around working with them and give you the confidence you need to start (or continue) your crystal journey.

We begin, in Part 1, with a look at what crystals are and how they work, before going on to choosing, caring for and programming them and, of course, how to go about using them. Then, in Part 2, we go deeper into the many areas in which crystals work their magic, whether you need to strengthen relationships, improve your sleep, be supported in your work or business, and so much more.

My aim is to support, guide and empower you in many different areas of your life. But, as the title of the book suggests, I also want you to treat the time you spend with your crystals as an act of self-care – a conscious undertaking to look after your own wellbeing and deliberately take care of your physical, emotional, mental and spiritual health. You are worth the same love, care and attention you give to everyone else around you and I want you to remember and honour that.

Block out the time you allocate to working with your crystals in the same way that you would a meeting. Commit to healing, growing and making improvements and changes in your life, wherever they are needed. You might choose to dedicate ten minutes a day to your self-care with crystals, or perhaps an hour once a week. Try working with the same crystals and areas for a few weeks before moving on, so that you can go deeper each time and really start to feel the benefits.

If you wear or carry your crystals daily, take a moment to connect with them as you put them on or into your pocket. See this in itself as an act of self-care as you allow them to infuse you with their energies all through the day.

◆ Keeping a Crystal Journal ◆

You may choose to keep a crystal journal so that you can make a note of the crystals you use and wear, grid with and manifest with for self-care. This will help you to notice any changes and magic taking place.

Finally, one thing I want to make clear right from the outset is that you are your own authority, and you know what is best for you. With crystals having grown in popularity, you will find countless well-meaning people telling you a thousand different things, but your journey with crystals is yours and yours alone. And while it's extremely useful in the beginning to take advice on things like the crystals that may be best for you or how they should be worn, over time, you will learn to trust in your own intuition and work with them on a much deeper, more personal level in a way that is right for you. I am here to help you with these things and more. This is where the real magic starts.

PART 1:

The Enchanted World of Crystals

In my experience, the thing that prevents many people from starting to work with crystals is the feeling that they don't understand what they are, how they work or what they should do with them. I want to answer all of those questions – and more – here, in Part 1. I will provide you with the basics about choosing, caring for, cleansing, charging and, ultimately, working with your crystals. I'll also share with you my go-to crystal kit and explain some of the terminology used in these pages, so that you will have a good understanding of all things crystals.

Let the journey begin . . .

CHAPTER 1

Crystals: A Quick Guide to What They Are and How They Work

In simple terms, crystals are an established batch of molecules and atoms that bond in a repeating pattern. They form over millions of years in a chemical process, during which movement in the earth's crust forces molten magma, liquids and gases towards the surface where they cool, solidify and crystallise. Crystals exist in many different shapes and colours, determined by their chemical components and bonds.

Did you know that it's a crystal that helps your phone, watch and TV to work? With very few legitimate studies done, science has yet to back the healing properties of crystals but what science can agree on is that crystals such as quartz produce energy. It's what's known as piezoelectricity and was discovered in 1880 by Jacques and Pierre Curie when they put crystals such as quartz, topaz and tourmaline under pressure and created electrical energy.

Science also agrees that everything is made of energy. Right now your energetic system is receiving and responding to all of the vibrations of energy not only in but around you.

◆ Crystal Energy ◆

I will talk about energies a lot in this book. If this is new to you, let me explain what I mean in brief, so that you can deepen your understanding of your own energies and, in turn, how the energy of crystals works.

Everything in the world is made of energy – you, your thoughts, your emotions and beliefs – and it is all vibrating to a particular frequency. Crystals, too, are made up of energies and, similarly, vibrate at a certain frequency. Working with them allows us to match our own energies and frequency with theirs, so that we can take advantage of their therapeutic properties, helping to soothe our emotions, calm our minds and bring ourselves back into balance and alignment.

When we speak of your energetic system, we are referring to your aura and your chakras.

◆ About Your Aura ◆

Have you ever just known that a friend is off or not feeling great without them saying anything, even when they try to tell you that everything is ok? That is you picking up on their subtle energy. Your aura reflects your emotions, thoughts, moods, energy levels and overall vibe. It is felt, rather than seen, and it is often someone's aura that we pick up on when we first meet them.

The aura is made up of seven different layers, each associated with different qualities (physical, emotional, mental, astral, spiritual, causal and true self).

◆ About Your Chakras ◆

Often described as your inner universe, your chakras are energy centres in the body that are constantly receiving and processing information from the world around you. There are seven main chakras, each relating to a different area of the body and aspect of our being. They are: root (safety), sacral (emotions), solar plexus (power), heart (love), throat (communication), third eye (intuition) and crown (connection). They are explained in more detail in Chapter 6 ('Crystals for . . . the Chakras').

◆ The Power of Crystals ◆

When the energies in our physical, energetic, mental, emotional or spiritual bodies become blocked, stagnant, stuck or overactive, we begin to feel out of alignment and disconnected, and things in our lives don't seem to flow or work as well as they could. This is where the power of crystals comes in.

Every crystal has its own geometric pattern that is repeated over and over, so that each one holds its own energy and vibrates to a specific frequency. Whereas our human energies are in a constant state of flux, the energy frequency of crystals is stable, i.e. they emit the same energies at all times. So when we work with them, they can help to heal and restore balance in our own energies, lowering or raising our vibrations to match theirs, absorbing, transforming and releasing stuck energies and bringing us back into alignment and balance where needed.

It is the unique energetic blueprint of each crystal that enables them to offer support, guidance and healing in different areas of your life. Some will work with the energy of your heart and any healing that needs to take place there; some will clear blockages you have around money and abundance; some will help you to find your voice and speak your truth; and some will soothe your anxieties and work to keep you calm in challenging situations. Certain crystals will bring you strength and protection, while others will help you to be more open and receiving. Again, it is useful to think of crystals as friends who are on your team and want to help you in the best way that they can.

We all have our own skills and strengths and things we are naturally good at as part of our energetic make-up, and it's the same with crystals. We choose or are drawn to (you might say chosen by) the crystals we need to balance our energies.

Holding, wearing and placing particular crystals on your body and around your home allows you to connect to their energies, enabling them to do their work of aligning and regulating your energies and supporting you in the very best way that a crystal knows how.

◆ Your Go-to Crystal Kit ◆

Before we go any further, here are my crystal must-haves:

Clear quartz
Known as the master crystal, this is one of the most popular and versatile crystals and is known for its high vibrations. Clear quartz helps to amplify (thoughts,

words, intentions and more – whatever you ask it to work with), and so it's amazing to use for manifesting or intention setting, and when you want to raise your own vibration. Clear quartz can balance all the chakras and bring mental, spiritual and emotional clarity, aiding you in getting clear on the direction of your life.

Clear quartz can be used and programmed for just about anything, and so if you don't have any of the crystals mentioned in Part 2 of the book, you can use a clear quartz in their place and program it to do the work you want it to do. It's also good for enhancing the energy of other crystals, so keep a clear quartz tumbled stone or point with any other crystals you are working with to increase their energy and power.

Rose quartz

The crystal of universal, unconditional love. Everyone needs to own a rose quartz. Rose quartz will lend a helping crystal hand in all matters of the heart. Whether that's finding self-love and self-worth, healing or opening your heart, embracing forgiveness, discovering a new relationship, healing from on old one or deepening the love in an existing one, rose quartz will help to invite more love into your life.

Moonstone

Given my love affair with the moon, this is obviously one of my favourites! As its name suggests, moonstone helps us to connect to lunar cycles, the feminine realms of intuition and the understanding that life is all about cycles and rhythm and flow. Moonstone can calm the emotions and is known as the crystal of new beginnings – it is powerful in any times of change.

Citrine

The crystal of abundance, citrine is your go-to when it comes to manifesting, prosperity and wealth. Highly energising, it's good for confidence, inner power and self-esteem. It's like the joyous friend who immediately lifts your mood and makes you smile and believe in yourself.

Amethyst

Bringing peaceful and calm vibes and a whole host of magical superpowers, amethyst needs to be on your team. It will support you through difficult emotions, calm and bring clarity to your mind, help with sleep issues and connect you to higher guidance.

Black tourmaline

One of the best crystals for grounding and protection, black tourmaline can energetically shield and protect you, cleansing you and your environment. It will help to ground and connect you to the earth in any times of mental or emotional anxiety and release any heavy or unwanted energies.

Ethical crystals

As crystals have gained in popularity over the last few years, much more has come to light on how they are mined and also on their environmental impact (crystals are a non-renewable source and their extraction has been linked to labour issues and damage to the environment). If you already have some crystals, I would encourage you to work with those before rushing out to buy more; the crystals you have chose you for a reason, and you only need a small collection to get big results. When you do purchase crystals, please look for ethical suppliers; a good one should be able to tell you exactly where the crystals have been sourced from and many nowadays will only deal with mines they can visit. Ethical crystals may cost a little more, but by purchasing them, you ensure that you are supporting ethical mines and practices.

It's better to have five sustainably sourced crystals to work with than a houseful of hundreds of cheap and more readily available ones.

Key crystal terminology

Here is a list of some of the terminology used in this book:

❖ **Intention setting:** the act of stating what you intend to achieve, accomplish, create and bring into your life.

❖ **Manifesting:** the art of creating what you want in life through your actions, thoughts, beliefs and emotions.

❖ **Vibrations:** all things in the universe vibrate with energy and to a certain frequency, including us and all our thoughts, emotions and attitudes – and crystals, too, of course. The more positive the energy, the higher the vibe, so things like love, gratitude or kindness vibrate at a much higher frequency than fear, anxiety or doubt.

❖ **Crystal grids:** the placing of crystals in an intentional way to direct the energy towards a specific intention or focus.

❖ **Altar:** a sacred space that is dedicated to your personal growth or spiritual work; it becomes a visual focus for your intentions, manifestations and energy and a place you can go to daily to check in.

❖ **Corners:** the practice of feng shui holds that there is an energy map in your home connected to different areas or aspects of your life; depending on your intentions, you can add more power to them by setting up a crystal grid in specific spaces (it is not recommended to work with more than two or three areas at once).

CHAPTER 2:

Choosing Your Crystals (or Letting Them Choose You)

There are two ways to select your crystals: either you choose them or they choose you!

If you are seeking out crystals, you will likely have a specific purpose in mind for them, and so you would find ones that hold the properties you are looking for. Part 2 of the book goes into much more detail about this and should help you with all that you need to know about choosing the crystal that is right for you.

The other approach is to let the crystal pick you. It can sometimes take a little longer to get comfortable with this method, as it requires tuning into and trusting your intuition. The more you work with crystals, the more you will connect to that part of yourself and the easier this method will become.

You may find that as soon as you enter a crystal shop, a certain one just jumps out at you (figuratively, that is) and you just know that's the one. Otherwise, take a few long, slow, deep breaths. Open yourself up to 'feeling' the crystals and allow yourself to wander around and explore. You may be drawn to a certain colour or shape or you may feel that a particular crystal 'speaks' to you. Try holding a couple in your hand, one at a time. As you hold each one close your eyes and ask yourself how each one feels to you. Does it seem warm or heavy? Can you feel any differences between them – in their texture or energies? Some people feel a tingle in their hands or a warm feeling in their heart; or, for you, it may be a little voice that says 'Yes'.

For me, as soon as I hold a crystal, I know whether it's for me or not. If it's right, holding it feels like home; it feels as though it was always meant to be mine. You know that feeling you get when you meet someone, and you just know that you like their energy and vibe, and that they will be good for you? Well, it's the same with crystals.

It's also possible that in the beginning you feel nothing at all – and that's ok, too. Keep working with sensing crystal energies and it will become much more familiar over time.

One tip here is to get to know the feeling of your own energy first – and especially the energy in your hands:

❖ Rub the palms of your hands together, until they feel warm.

❖ Next, close your eyes and move your palms to about shoulder-distance apart, facing each other.

❖ Slowly move your palms closer together, until you feel a slight resistance between your hands – this is your energy field.

❖ You can experiment with moving your hands closer together and further apart to really feel this or imagine you are making an energy ball by moulding the energy between your hands into a ball shape.

Try your hand

You can also begin to tune into which hand is your receiving hand and which is your sending hand. Typically, your dominant hand (the one you write with) tends to be the one through which you release and send energy out into the world. Your non-dominant hand would be the hand through which you receive energies, and the one with which you would hold crystals to sense and accept their powers. Try holding a crystal first in one hand and then the other to see how it feels. It helps to know this for when you are meditating with your crystals, so you can hold the crystal in the relevant hand, depending on whether your intent through meditation is to receive energies, advice and guidance or to release stuck energy, emotion or fears. (See 'Crystals for Meditation', p. 38.)

You can apply a similar process when buying crystals; online. Take some time to look through the different images and see which one seems to jump off the page or keeps drawing you back. Once you have selected your crystal type, feel free to message the supplier and ask for pictures of different ones. So if you know, for example, that you want a citrine point, you can ask for pictures of five different ones, so you can choose the particular one that you want. This is how I buy crystals online and any good supplier should agree to this, so that you can see which speaks to you most.

Be discerning with where you purchase your crystals; there is no such thing as a 'bad' crystal, but there can be less-than-ethical suppliers (see p. 11). I tend to choose dedicated crystal shops and I generally find that as soon as I enter a shop or see a crystal stall or supplier online, I know if they seem legitimate. I want to buy from someone who is passionate about crystals and treats them well, and you can tell a lot from how the energy of the crystals and the shop feels – they should feel alive and vibrant, rather than numb or lifeless.

It's also worth remembering that it's always better to

start off with fewer crystals – say, three to five – and to do the work with them, instead of buying and trying to work with lots and lots, which can become overwhelming. You may try working with your chosen crystal for 30 days to really deepen the relationship and get the benefits, rather than swapping and changing every day. The more you connect to and spend time with your crystals, the more magic you will create together.

◆ Crystals as Gifts ◆

Gifting crystals to others is a beautiful thing to do and I'm often asked how to go about it.

Try holding the person in your mind's eye and feel into your heart what you would like the crystal to help them with – what is the purpose or intent behind this gift? You may want to look through the various chapters in this book and choose crystals based on what is going on in that person's life or keep them in mind when you are crystal shopping and then trust in your intuition.

I sometimes find that when I am crystal shopping, a certain person will come so clearly into my mind when I am near or holding a particular crystal and I will just know that it is intended for them. I have also bought crystals for myself in the past, got them home and realised they were not for me, after all, because our energies just didn't blend together, but that I knew just who they would be better suited to.

I often gift crystal pouches that contain four or five tumbled (see p. 23) stones for different purposes, so that the person can use different crystals at different times, based on what they are feeling drawn to.

◆ Crystal Shapes and Colours ◆

Crystals come in many different forms, shapes and sizes that will determine how you can use them.

Colour me beautiful

We'll explore more on colours and the chakras and how you can use different-coloured crystals in various areas of your life in Part 2, but for now, here is a rough guide to what the colours of crystals mean:

❧ **Black** – grounding and protection

❧ **Brown** – support and nourishment

❧ **Red (root chakra)** – energy and action

❧ **Orange (sacral chakra)** – change and creativity

22

❖ **Yellow (solar-plexus chakra)** – power and optimism

❖ **Pink (heart chakra)** – love and acceptance

❖ **Green (heart chakra)** – growth and abundance

❖ **Light blue (throat chakra)** – communication and wisdom

❖ **Deep blue/indigo (third-eye chakra)** – clarity and intuition

❖ **Violet/purple (crown chakra)** – awakening and spirituality

❖ **White or clear (all chakras)** – cleansing and purifying

Shaping up

When it comes to crystal shapes, some are natural and others are man-made and have been cut to shape. Here are some of the most common:

❖ **Tumbled:** The most common and versatile type of crystal, this is when small crystals are polished in a special machine until they become smooth and shiny. These can be carried, held or used in grids or for just about any purpose.

❦ **Raw:** Sometimes known as chunks, these are often larger pieces of crystal in their natural form. Raw crystals are frequently used in grids, within rooms to help with the environment or are held during meditation.

❦ **Cluster:** A number of smaller crystals (usually points) in their natural form that join together and are attached to the same matrix. Clusters are good for radiating energy into a room or environment.

❦ **Points:** Usually naturally occurring, with a rough base where the crystal has been removed from its matrix. They can focus and direct energy and are great to use when meditating or manifesting.

❦ **Spheres:** Shaped into a sphere or a circle, as the name suggests, these are a good focal point for meditation or to soothe in times of stress. They bring harmony and allow energy to radiate in all directions, while creating a sense of wholeness and a reminder that you are connected to something greater – like you are holding the whole world in your hand.

❖ **Pyramids:** Shaped into a pyramid, these are amazing for manifesting what you want and connecting to high-vibration energies and higher consciousness.

❖ **Wands:** These are usually pointed at one end and rounded at the other, although you can get double-terminated wands with a point at each end. Wands are used for healing and to release negative energy or bring healing energy into the body.

❖ **Towers:** Usually carved/polished into shape, so that they stand up, these are similar to a point in that they help to direct and focus energy.

Now that you've chosen your crystal/s, it's time to go a little deeper . . .

CHAPTER 3:

Caring for and Programming Your Crystals

With your crystal collection under way, it's time to learn how to take care of them. Crystals tend to be fairly low-maintenance but, just like people, a little TLC is needed to get the best out of them.

◆ Cleansing and Charging Your Crystals ◆

Your crystals may have been on quite a journey to get to you, often crossing continents and passing through many hands. So the first thing you'll want to do with your new crystals is to cleanse them.

As we've learned, crystals hold vibrational energy. If you imagine your crystals as an air filter, they are working to cleanse, purify, transform and raise the quality of the vibrations all around them, while filtering out all the lower or unnecessary ones. Just as an air filter needs changing every once in a while, to do its best work, the same goes for your crystals.

It is important to mention that there is a difference between *cleansing* and *charging* your crystals. While cleansing helps to remove unwanted energies from your crystals, at times, they might also need a bit of charging; just like your mobile phone or laptop battery, your crystals' energy may drain if they've been hard at work, so remember to charge them up once in a while.

Here are some ways to treat your crystals to some cleansing/charging care:

❖ **Moonlight:** The light of the full moon will not only cleanse, but also charge your crystals, bringing them back to their full power. On the night of a full moon, simply lay your crystals outside if you can – they especially love to be on the earth. If that's not possible, a window ledge or balcony where they can soak up the moonbeams will do just fine. It doesn't matter if it's a cloudy evening, or even if you can't see the moon, they will still absorb the lunar vibes. And it also doesn't matter if you miss the night of the full moon; the night before or after will also work.

❖ **Sunlight:** Most people tend to charge their crystals by the moon, but there is nothing nicer than putting them out on a warm, sunny day. Just like the moon, the beams of the sun will cleanse and charge your crystals, filling them with more light and life. Place your crystals on the earth outside for a little sunbathing time or, again, on a window ledge or balcony. Just be mindful that some crystals can fade and/or crack if placed under intense direct sunlight for too long (pink and purple ones especially), so don't leave them out all day – an hour or so of sunshine should be more than enough.

❖ **Water:** You can soak or run your crystals under running water, while visualising washing them clean of any energy they no longer need. I often used to take my crystals to a local stream and treat them to fresh running water. Please be mindful, however, that many crystals are water-soluble and so should not be placed in water. As a general rule, those that end in -*ite* should not get wet (for example, selenite, hematite, celestite, malachite, angelite, etc.).

❖ **A crystal bed:** Place your crystals on a bed of amethyst or clear quartz. Every night, I put the crystal jewellery I've worn on a large bed of amethyst, so that it can be cleansed overnight.

Selenite is also amazing for charging other crystals, so you can keep your other crystals by a piece of selenite.

- **Smudging/smoke:** Use sage, Palo Santo or incense and waft the smoke over and around your crystals, visualising the smoke cleansing away any unwanted energies.

- **Energy healing:** You can use energy healing such as reiki to cleanse and charge your crystals. You would first hold the crystal with the intention of using reiki to cleanse it. Once you feel this has happened, you can charge the crystal back up using your healing vibes.

- **Earth:** Every now and then, you may find a crystal that wants to go back to the earth for a while, especially if you have been doing deep healing work together. If this happens (and it's usually just a feeling you get), bury your crystal in the earth for a few weeks to cleanse and charge it. Again, be mindful of water-soluble crystals, as they will likely get wet in the earth.

In the same way that we need to take care of ourselves, so that we have the energy to be able to help take care of others, our crystals sometimes need a little self-care and time out. After the initial cleansing when you get your crystals home you may want to cleanse/charge your crystals once a month or every so often. As you get to know them better, you'll know when it's time – when mine start to feel or look a little 'dull', I know it's time to treat them to some care.

◆ Programming Your Crystals ◆

With your crystals cleansed and charged, it's time to program them, so that they can heal, balance, align and amplify your own energy.

When I first get a crystal, I hold it in my hands and ask it to work with me for my highest good and the highest good of all. I do this out of respect for the crystal. In my opinion we don't own anything from the earth and crystals come to us to work *with* us, not *for* us. This needs to be a partnership and, just like human inter-actions, there needs to be a mutual respect. I like to treat my crystals as living vibrational beings who are going to work alongside me.

I then ask my crystals to be self-cleansing and self-charging – this does not mean that they don't ever need cleansing or charging, but just that they tend not to need it as often.

I also ask my crystal not to take on the energies of anyone else. This is particularly important, as you'll notice, especially when you are doing powerful work with a crystal, that people are drawn to it and want to hold it. This ensures that your crystal is protected from other people's energies.

CHAPTER 4:

How to Work with Crystals

You've chosen your crystals and they are cleansed, programmed and ready to go. So now what?

As we've explored, crystals already come with a purpose and the properties they are best used for, but it really helps to add to the energy and power of working with a particular crystal if you program it for what you especially want to use it for, adding an intention to working together (to help bring you love, soothe your anxiety or bring you your dream job, for example). This can focus the energy and allow the crystal to support you even more.

◆ One or Many? ◆

A frequently asked question is whether it's ok to use more than one crystal at a time, and the answer is yes . . . and no!

In truth, it depends on what your intention is for working with a number of crystals. If you are working to cleanse and balance your chakras, and you want a crystal for each one, then absolutely – as each will have its own purpose and job to do (and the same applies to crystal grids). You may want to meditate with a crystal in each hand or with one on your third eye (your forehead) and one on your heart. Again, this is more than ok, as each crystal will have its own purpose and is able to work with you in its own special way.

If, however, it's simply that you feel more is better and you want to throw all the crystals at a situation, that may not be the best idea. It's a bit like when you have more people working together, the energy may be more powerful – especially if they share similar working methods or goals; but if you have a roomful of people all wanting to make their voices heard and do things their own way, you may find it becomes more of a struggle than anything else and the bigger workforce is not beneficial at all.

If you do decide to work with more than one crystal, it's more useful either to choose a different crystal for each specific purpose (as with the chakras – see Chapter 6) or to find ones that complement each other energetically and will, together, bring more power to the work you are doing with them.

Just having crystals around your home is enough to benefit from them, especially if you set an intention on them (see below), as they will keep amplifying the intention and sending their vibes out into your environment. But you will likely want to go deeper – and so you should. As I said earlier, crystals are like friends and the more time you spend with them, the deeper the connection will be and the more you will benefit from their magic. We will cover more on specific meditations, intention setting and grids for different areas of your life in Part 2, but for now, here's a guide to the many ways you can work with your crystals daily.

◆ Intention Setting with Crystals ◆

I love to set intentions with my crystals and use them to help me to manifest what I want. When you set an intention with a crystal, it will continue to amplify the energies of that intention, working to draw it more quickly into your life.

I usually set intentions around the lunar cycles as it holds more power (see Chapter 13) but you can set intentions at any time.

I'm not sure if my publisher knows this, but I used intention setting with a crystal to manifest my first book, *Lunar Living*, when it was being presented to the wider team for a final decision on whether we would go ahead. The day before the presentation, I held a moonstone and asked for its assistance in getting the book deal. I visualised not only the 'Yes', but also how it would feel to have my book out in the world. I asked for help to spread the word of my passion for living in alignment with lunar cycles and moon magic, filling that little crystal with all my hopes and dreams for the book and asking it to please send these energies to everyone involved in making the decision. I then hid the moonstone in the bushes outside my publishing company Yellow Kite's offices. I must admit, looking back now, the sight of a girl skulking around, trying to hide a crystal in the bushes must have been so strange. But it worked! They said yes, *Lunar Living* was brought into the world and it became a *Sunday Times* bestseller. And to this day, there is a crystal hidden in the bushes outside my publisher's offices sending out good vibes! If you want to try this same intention-setting magic for yourself, here's how to do it:

1. Take some time to consider why you have chosen the particular crystal you are using, and the support you really want from it. Get as specific as you can. For example: if you want to bring love into your life, what kind of love would that be? If you want help with a new job or a career choice, what would that look or feel

like? Maybe you want to feel calmer and more relaxed, and that would come through not over-thinking or worrying about the future quite as much. The clearer you can be on what you want your crystal to work on, the better.

2. Next, try to distil this into a sentence or two. For example:

❖ 'I ask that you please help me to find a love that is honest and true. I ask that you help release any blocks or fears around receiving love and open me up to the right person coming into my life.'

❖ 'I ask that you help me to find a job that is fulfilling and satisfying. A job where I can best use my skills and experience and be appreciated for all that I do.'

❖ 'I ask that you please help bring more peace and tranquillity into my life. I ask that you help me to calm my mind and remain more focused in the present moment.'

When you have come up with your sentence/s, hold your crystal in your hand (either or both hands) or even against your heart, and say your intention out loud or whisper it from your heart.

3. You can then wear your crystal or keep it in a special place or on an altar, where it will continue to emit the relevant vibrations for you at all times, even when you're not together; and each time you hold, meditate or work with your crystal, the same intention will be amplified.

◆ Crystals for Meditation ◆

Crystals can transform your meditation experience. There are a number of ways and reasons for choosing to meditate with crystals, from helping to quieten your mind and connecting you with your deep inner wisdom to accessing your higher self, manifesting or amplifying your intentions and working to shift your energies if you are overwhelmed, stressed or feeling like you need a little more get up and go. Your crystals will guide and support you in what you need.

◆ Three easy ways to ◆ meditate with crystals

1. **Hold them in your hand/s:** Feel the energy exchange between you and the crystal and allow it to work with you during your meditation

practice. Hold the crystal, close your eyes and visualise it doing the work of helping you to release or draw to you what you need. You may remember that we talked earlier about discovering your sending and receiving hands – see p. 20.) This comes in really useful during meditation with crystals, as it will help you to direct the energies even more powerfully. If I have been feeling stressed, anxious and overwhelmed and my intention during meditating with my crystals is to release those feelings, I will hold the relevant crystal in my releasing hand and allow it to support me in letting go of anything I don't need. If I am working on manifesting something, or needing to receive extra energies or guidance, I will hold the crystal in my receiving hand to allow these energies to come into my being.

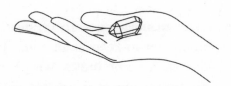

2. **Place them on your body:** You may feel that your heart needs a little healing, that your throat needs opening (if you've been struggling to

communicate your needs) or that you want to add a little more power to your solar plexus (if you've been giving away your power and not maintaining clear boundaries). If so, lie down, place the relevant crystals over the relevant places on your body (see p. 58) and close your eyes, while the crystals do their work. Stay like this for ten minutes, or until you feel a difference in the area/s concerned.

3. **Create an energy field:** You might want the energy and support of your crystals, but not want to hold or place them on your body. In this case, you can place them in a circle around you, or just one in front of and one behind you, so they can still hold and support you in their energies. Sit or lie for as long as you would do your usual meditation while you soak in their energies.

It's also powerful to meditate with crystals that you have set intentions on to keep amplifying them, and you may find guidance coming to you through the meditation. You can use any of the above options to do this or sit in front of the special place or altar where you have placed your crystals and tune into their energies before and after the meditation.

◆ Crystal Grids ◆
and How to Use Them

Put simply, a crystal grid is an arrangement of crystals used with intention to manifest a desired result. As we learned in the intention-setting section above, when you set an intention on crystals, they continue to amplify this, and when you grid them it creates an even more powerful energy vortex. Using crystal grids is exceptionally effective, as your crystals continue to work on your intention at all times and, as such, they should definitely be part of your work with crystals.

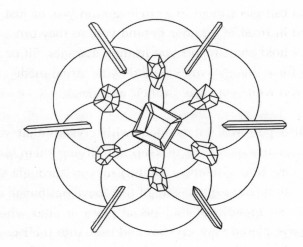

Traditionally, crystal grids were used with sacred geometry an ancient science that explores the energy patterns and shapes that exist in nature all around us, as it was believed this increased their power. In some cases, I have found this to be true, while in others, I prefer to follow my own guidance. You can have crystal grids around your house for protection, love or abundance, or you may set one up before a big interview or date. Before I appeared on *This Morning* over Skype, for example, I gridded my laptop with crystals to ensure that my message of moon magic would be delivered to the nation in the best way possible.

There really is no right or wrong with crystal grids, and as you get more confident with using them, you'll realise there are no limits to how they can be utilised. Use them for just about any dream, goal or intention that you want to manifest to know that you have crystal power right behind you. On the Leo New Moon Lionsgate Portal in 2021 I set an intention to start to let myself shine and be seen in my business so that I could make more of a difference in the world, placing my written intention under a crystal grid. Two weeks later, on the full blue moon, my book became a *Sunday Times* bestseller again. I'll let you know when the other intentions under my crystal grid come true, as I am sure they will, but this is the power of setting your intentions with a crystal grid, especially with a little moon magic thrown in too.

Your ten-step beginner's guide to setting up a crystal grid

1. The most important thing is the intention behind your grid and holding that clear intention as you set it up. So get very clear on what this is – I would suggest you write it down. As long as your intention/s is/are there, the grid will work as it is intended.

2. Choose a centre crystal. It's a good idea to ensure this is one that resonates with the intention of your grid (i.e. love, abundance, communication) – or you can use a quartz point for directing your intention. This is also known as the anchor stone, as it anchors the intention of your grid.

3. Choose the rest of your crystals based on the purpose and intention of your grid, but also feel free to add any extra crystals that you are drawn to using.

4. You may also want to add quartz points to your grid to activate the flow of energy. Points facing in will bring more of what you intend in, while points facing out will help to release anything in the way or that needs to go.

5. Cleanse your crystals and the space you are going to set up the grid using Palo Santo, sage, incense or energy healing.

6. Place your centre/anchor crystal in the middle of your grid. You can also place the piece of paper you wrote your intention on underneath it.

7. Place the rest of your crystals in your chosen shape or sacred geometric pattern (you can – but don't have to – purchase special boards or cloths for this) around your central crystal. Keep your intention in mind as you do this and feel as though all the crystals are connecting to create one big energy grid. A simple beginner's grid would be a circle of crystals placed around your anchor crystal and then possibly an outer circle around that. As you get more confident with gridding, you will be guided by what feels right.

8. If you feel you want to, you can add candles, flower petals, leaves, images, statues or anything else that represents what your grid is all about.

9. Activate your grid. I like to use a quartz point for this. Starting at the centre, touch your point to your anchor crystal, then using the point

energetically, draw a line from crystal to crystal to join them all to each other – a bit like connect-the-dots.

10. Leave your grid in place for as long as you want. I usually recommend at least one lunar cycle, but I have grids that remain in place all the time (for things that I want to keep in my life – like abundance or protection).

Have a play around with different crystals and ways of setting up your grid, until it feels right for you, and enjoy the process of discovery.

◆ Self-Care Crystal Grids ◆

For some deep healing self-care time, you can also create crystal grids on and around your body. I would suggest lying in a grid of crystals with one at your crown, one by your feet and, perhaps, others by your shoulders, hips and knees. You can also place crystals on your chakras or hold them in your hands to really soak in their healing qualities. A crystal grid will surround you with powerful energetic healing, working on you physically, mentally, emotionally and spiritually. Different ways of doing this will be covered in Part 2.

◆ Wearing Your Crystals ◆

One of the simplest ways to connect with the energies of your chosen crystal daily is to wear it, most commonly in the form of jewellery like necklaces, rings and bracelets. I find it so comforting to wear my crystal every day and often find myself holding it without realising, especially when I need guidance or support. You can buy jewellery ready-made or purchase little wire holders that you can place any crystal in yourself. Alternatively, many crystal shops and suppliers can wire wrap your chosen crystal for you. You can even wear them in your bra if you want them to be really close!

◆ Holding Crystals for Support ◆

Finally, you can choose to simply hold crystals and take a few long, slow, deep breaths to connect with their energies whenever you need to. I have a piece of lemurian quartz to allow me to connect to a higher wisdom and knowledge, and I hold it when I record a meditation or deliver a workshop, Instagram Live or coaching session. Other times, I may hold a piece of rose quartz if I need to connect to my heart or black tourmaline if I need to ground. Those few moments of purposefully connecting your energy with your crystals may be all you need to set you up for the rest of the day.

CHAPTER 5:

Time to Say Goodbye

Just as with any relationship in life, there may be times when your work with your crystal is done and your journey together has come to an end. Crystals often know much sooner when this is than we do; as humans, we are never very good at endings and letting go. When this happens your crystal may break, or just simply disappear. It is sad, but please don't see it as a sign of anything bad. Your crystal just loved you enough to know when it was time to let go.

I used to have a piece of angelite that would regularly disappear on me for months at a time and turn up in the strangest of places, like a dressing gown pocket, for example. It would always seem like it had showed up at exactly the right time as a reminder to reconnect back to my guides for the answers I was looking for. So if a crystal disappears, don't panic. It may be that it has done its work and taken itself away, or that it will show up again when you need its energy the most.

Crystals are often like little guardian angels turning up at just the right time, and in just the right way.

If a crystal breaks clean in half or into useable pieces, please continue to use it, trusting that it was meant to be in different pieces to do its best work. I once bought a beautiful, large pink amethyst geode and as soon as I took it out of the packaging, it leaped out of my hands, on to the table, and broke into two pieces. I had a human moment of being so upset, but then I realised that's how this crystal had always meant to come to me. It looked perfect in its two parts and I could no longer imagine it whole. Now I have one piece in the bedroom and one in the living room, so its energies fill more of my home.

If a crystal completely shatters, I see it as a sign that the work we did together is completed, the lessons are learned, the blockages are released, the issues have been worked through. Even if you can't see any physical manifestation of the work just yet, trust and believe that the work this crystal was doing with you has happened. And please don't panic, thinking that a broken crystal means that any areas of your life you were working on with it are broken, too; they are not. It just means that the crystal has done what it needed to do in relation to that life area and it may be that you now need another one with a slightly different purpose to take you further, or just that you need to be patient and allow the magic to unfold. It is the crystal's time to return to the earth, so I give love and gratitude for the work we did together and bury broken crystals back in the ground.

Alternatively, it might be you who feels as though your journey with a crystal has come to an end. You may not be drawn to hold or use your crystal any more or feel the same vibes from it as you once did, and this too is ok. In fact, it's more than ok, as it shows that on some level you know you have healed or learned or experienced what you needed to with this crystal.

Crystals come in and out of our lives to teach us what they need to teach us. When this happens, consider gifting your crystal to someone else. Just because it has finished its work with you, that's not to say it doesn't still have work to do with someone else. You may sit and hold the crystal and see who comes to mind or notice if any of your friends speak to you about issues you know this crystal would be beneficial for. Very often, the crystal/universe will help you to guide it to exactly the right place. Then cleanse your crystal, take a moment to give thanks for the journey and maybe even reflect on any lessons learned, before sending it with love to its new home to continue its magic.

◆　◆　◆

Now we've learned all we need to know about choosing, caring for, cleansing, programming and, of course, working with your crystals, let's move on to Part 2 to see how you can bring the power and magic of crystals into all the different areas of your life.

PART 2:

Making Crystals a Part of Your Life

Next, we are going to move into how to use the magic of crystals to support you in all different spheres of your life.

This section covers all the main life areas that I am asked frequently about, along with those that I have personally used crystals in over the years. Within each section I offer suggestions for the different crystals and recommended colours to use, as well as the related chakras to work with. I also provide ideas for meditations, visualisations, affirmations, grids and ways in which to deepen your crystal magic in each area.

There may be days when you need gentle soothing and other days when you need a little more of a kick in the right direction, and you will learn which crystal holds the energy for what you need. You will also find that the more you work with your chosen crystals, the deeper your connection with them and the more they can work with you. Over time, you will learn to trust in the wisdom of your body, energy and intuition and begin to know the best crystal for you in times of need.

Remember that it's better to begin with just a small selection of crystals (see p. 33). And with this in mind, I have tried, where possible, to use the same crystals in a few different sections, so that you can get the most out of them. Each holds a number of properties and so can be used for different things, depending on your needs.

CHAPTER 6:

Crystals for . . .
the Chakras

We've touched on chakras already, but here we're going to go much deeper into what they are and how we can work with them. So let's get a brief understanding of them before we go any further.

Chakras are energy centres within the body. Often described as a spinning wheel of energy that is continually receiving, processing and expressing information from the world in and around us, there are seven main chakras in the body, and each relates to a different physical, emotional, psychological and spiritual aspect of our being.

The chakras are our inner universe and help to keep us balanced in body, mind, heart and soul. Just like crystals, each chakra vibrates to its own energy frequency and spins at its own pace. When our chakras are balanced and aligned, we feel connected to ourselves and in flow with life. However, they can begin to spin out of balance and, when they do, we tend to feel stuck, stagnant or closed off in certain areas of ourselves and our lives. Using crystals is a wonderful way to balance the energies in your body and bring your chakras back into alignment.

If you are feeling out of alignment in any of the areas associated with a particular chakra, it may be time for a little crystal TLC. Each chakra is associated with a different colour, and so one of the simplest ways to use crystals with your chakras is by using one that's the same colour as the chakra you want to balance.

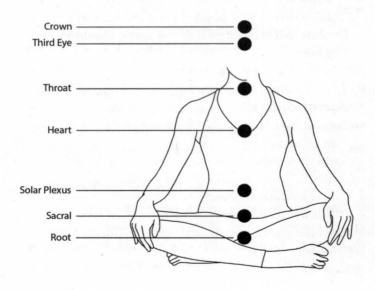

Or, if you want to go deeper into a particular area, you could also use crystals specific to what each chakra is associated with. We will cover all this in more detail in the following chapters. For now, here are some suggested crystals and a bit more information about each chakra to get you started.

Root chakra

Located: at the base of the spine

Colour: red

Associated with: feeling grounded, safe and secure in life; having all of your basic needs met – from physical to financial and emotional; feeling connected to your physical body and the earth

Crystals: red crystals, such as red jasper, bloodstone or garnet

---

Sacral chakra

Located: just beneath the belly button

Colour: orange

Associated with: emotional wellbeing and regulation; the ability to feel and process your feelings; relationships and sexuality and how we relate to others; creativity, pleasure, play and enjoyment of life

Crystals: orange crystals, such as carnelian, fire opal or amber

---

Solar-plexus chakra

Located: just beneath the rib cage

Colour: yellow

Associated with: your personal power, beliefs and identity; drive, willpower and taking control of the direction of your life and being able to trust and follow your own guidance

Crystals: yellow crystals, such as citrine, tiger's eye or yellow jasper

Heart chakra

Located: in the centre of the chest

Colour: pink or green

Associated with: all forms of love, from self-love to love for others; acceptance and forgiveness; connection to life and the world around you

Crystals: pink crystals, such as rose quartz or kunzite; green crystals such as jade and aventurine

Throat chakra

Located: at the base of the throat

Colour: light blue

Associated with: communication and your ability to express yourself and your needs and desires; staying true to yourself and speaking your truth

Crystals: blue crystals, such as blue lace agate, lapis lazuli or kyanite

Third-eye chakra

Located: on the forehead, just above and between the eyebrows

Colour: indigo

Associated with: intuition and spiritual awareness; being able to 'see' beyond what the physical eyes can see and vision the future; inner wisdom and knowing

Crystals: indigo crystals, such as sodalite, azurite or labradorite

Crown chakra

Located: at the crown of your head

Colour: violet

Associated with: consciousness and connection to higher guidance, the universe and divine (or whatever name you give to it) unity

Crystals: violet/purple crystals, such as amethyst, sugilite and lepidolite

Note: clear/white crystals, such as clear quartz, selenite and apophyllite, are also sometimes associated with the crown chakra, but can also be used to balance all of the chakras.

◆ Crystal Chakra Meditation ◆

One of the simplest ways to bring your chakras back into balance using crystals is to enjoy a crystal chakra meditation. Simply choose a corresponding-coloured crystal for one or every chakra, lie down comfortably and place the relevant crystal on the appropriate chakra, as follows:

- ❧ **Root:** just above the pubic bone or off the body between the legs

- ❧ **Sacral:** between the hip bones, just beneath the belly button

- ❧ **Solar plexus:** between the lower ribs and belly button

- ❧ **Heart:** at the centre of your chest

- ❧ **Throat:** at the base of your throat

- ❧ **Third eye:** between the eyebrows

- ❧ **Crown:** off the body right above your head

You may follow a guided meditation, set a timer for 10–15 minutes or play some relaxing music, as you focus on your breathing: take really long, slow, deep breaths, following the flow of your inhale and exhale; visualise bringing energy into your chakras with each inhale and releasing anything that is blocked or stuck with each exhale. You could also visualise each chakra – one at a time, for a few breaths from the root to the crown – and feel the healing energy of the crystals doing their work and each chakra cleansing and balancing.

If a crystal falls off during the meditation, don't worry – it doesn't mean it's not working. Just replace it, if that feels right, or leave it. It's your choice; you can't get this wrong. However, I would say that if you replace it and it falls off a second time, it's best to leave it and trust that the energy and crystals know what they are doing and that chakra has got what it needed.

Make sure that you cleanse your crystals (see p. 27) after you have finished. You can enjoy this meditation as often as and whenever you like (maybe make it a weekly act of self-care), but especially when you feel out of sorts, out of balance or not aligned in yourself.

CHAPTER 7

Crystals for . . .
Love and Relationships

Crystals are one of your greatest companions when it comes to the journey of love. Whether it's for self-love, healing from love, welcoming love or deepening existing love, there is a crystal out there just waiting to support you.

I am going to give you lots of crystal ideas for love in this chapter, but you'll hear me mention rose quartz a lot, as it is the crystal of universal, unconditional love and is one of the best for whatever you need when it comes to love. You can also work with any pink and/ or green crystals, paying attention to or placing or wearing your chosen crystal over your heart chakra.

◆ Self-love ◆

It's impossible to truly love anyone else or allow anyone else to truly love you until you love yourself. If you ever struggle with self-love or lack of self-worth, self-care or not feeling worthy or deserving, rose quartz needs to become your best friend.

Rose quartz

Rose quartz carries a beautiful, loving, feminine energy that helps to heal and open your heart and allow love in. I would always suggest wearing rose quartz, especially when you begin your self-love or crystal journey, so that you can connect to those loving vibes at all times. If you can find a necklace that goes over your heart, even better.

Another powerful way to work with rose quartz is to hold a piece while repeating self-love affirmations, and if you can look at yourself in the mirror while doing this, it will be even more powerful. Set an intention on your piece of rose quartz for self-love and then hold it as you repeat your affirmations daily. These might include the following:

❖ 'I love and approve of myself.'

❖ 'I am perfect just as I am.'

❖ 'I am enough.'

Carry your rose quartz with you as a self-love reminder or put it in a special place throughout the day – perhaps even over a picture of yourself or in a grid (see p. 41 and below) – where it will continue to amplify your self-love vibes and bring you more self-love each time you connect with it.

Hold a piece of rose quartz in your receiving hand while you meditate and sense the energy of love flowing into and filling your entire body. Or lie back and place a piece of rose quartz on your heart chakra and feel the crystal lovingly and gently open your heart to more unconditional self-love.

Magnesite

One of my all-time favourite crystals is magnesite, a crystal that is so powerful for teaching you about self-love. It can remind you of your value and worth and instils a sense of confidence in you, allowing you to believe in and love yourself enough to create anything you desire in your life. It helps you to get to know and love the authentic you and, in doing so, ensures that you don't abandon or lose yourself – especially when it comes to relationships (this makes it an exceptional crystal for those of you who tend to do that). Carry around a piece of magnesite to feel the power of this soothing, loving crystal.

Self-love grids

In times when you really need to be infused with self-love you can create a self-love grid by surrounding yourself with pieces of rose quartz, magnesite, some quartz points and any of the crystals in this section. Place a piece of rose quartz over your heart and the others around your body, even holding one in each hand. I would suggest having some of the quartz points facing inwards to direct the flow of loving energy towards you, and you could even place a few turned out for releasing anything that stands in the way of you loving yourself fully and completely. Lie down within this grid for as long as you need to, soaking in the loving vibes. See this as time well spent, truly taking time for *you*, as an act of self-love and care.

Other crystals for self-love: rhodochrosite, rhodonite, carnelian and pink tourmaline.

◆ Healing from Love ◆

If you know that you have closed off your heart and that you have some healing to do from past relationships and hurts, crystals can help you not only to heal, but to provide powerful insights that will allow you to move on. You can carry any of the suggested crystals with you, holding them in times of need, or

64

meditate with them to take advantage of their powerful healing properties.

In times of real heartbreak or when you need some deep heart healing, lie down within a healing grid (as described in the self-love grid) but this time using the suggested crystals below. Place your quartz points facing out for the release of heartbreak, hurt and emotional wounds. As you lie there, bring your awareness to your heart and feel as though you are breathing in and out through your heart. Absorb the healing energies of the crystals into your heart with each inhale and, as you exhale, soften your heart, allowing any hurt, pain, anger, sadness or resentment to release and dissolve. Visualise the crystals holding and supporting you, surrounding you in healing and love and soothing your pain.

Rhodochrosite

If you find yourself in the same situations in love, over and over again, rhodochrosite will help you to learn your lessons. It's a wonderful crystal for moving on after rejection and working through any painful emotions without closing off your heart. This is also a powerful crystal if you need to forgive. Remember that forgiveness does not mean that you are saying what someone did was ok, but rather that you are no longer willing to carry it around in your heart. Rhodochrosite will help you to release the pain and open your heart to forgive both others and yourself, if needs be.

Malachite

Malachite is a powerful crystal for grief and heartbreak. It works with your heart, bringing deep emotional healing. It can also keep you out of the past and constantly wandering down the relationship memory lane, so allowing you to let go. Known as the transformation crystal, malachite will encourage you to take your heartbreak, learn from it and open your heart to a new relationship adventure when you are ready. It's incredibly powerful, so use with care. Perhaps work first with other, more gentle crystals – such as rose quartz or rhodochrosite (above) – moving on to malachite once you feel a little more emotionally stable and are ready for that push to move you forward into deep healing.

Apache tears

Wonderful crystals for grief, heartbreak or times of emotional crisis, ancient legend has it that apache tears were formed by a group of strong women mourning a huge loss, and that they cried enough tears for all those who mourn. This crystal brings a comforting, soothing energy, while helping you to heal emotional wounds and grieve the past or, as is often the case when a relationship ends, an imagined future.

Dioptase

This is one of the most supportive crystals for the heart, emotionally and spiritually. It is powerful for healing old wounds and resentment you have held on to when it comes to relationships. It helps you to find compassion (for yourself) and to forgive and let go, especially when there has been betrayal or abandonment. If you feel stuck in terms of love, in particular after past hurts, it is great for moving forward.

Other crystals for healing from love: Rose quartz, morganite, rainbow obsidian or pink amethyst (you may also want to try the letting-go exercise on p. 122).

◆ Welcoming in Love ◆

Crystals can be an incredible wing (wo)man when it comes to attracting love into your life.

One of the simplest ways is to take some time to get very clear on what you want from the relationship in question and write it all down. Then take a raw piece of rose quartz (but tumbled will do if it's all you have), hold the crystal to your heart and read your list to the crystal, asking for help in attracting this love to you. Once you have finished, place your rose quartz (with your love list underneath, if you wish) in the relationship corner of your home or bedroom – this is the farthest right-hand corner as you stand with your back to the door. Your rose quartz will then go to work in helping you to attract this love into your life. You can also create a crystal grid here for manifesting your love to you. To do so, add more rose quartz and/or the suggested crystals below to your central piece of rose quartz and, if you like, some clear quartz points – facing inwards – for drawing the love that you desire to you.

Or try setting intentions on the crystals below, asking them to support you in bringing the love you want and deserve into your life. You can hold them while you meditate to amplify your intentions and call that love into your life, or place them over your heart, feeling them open it, ready to receive this new love. Wearing or carrying them with you somewhere on your body, especially when out in social settings, will open you up more to the love you are looking for.

Pink amethyst

One of my favourite crystals for working with the heart and believing in love is the newly discovered pink amethyst. This beautiful-looking crystal radiates divine love that you can feel from simply looking at it and, to me, it feels as though I get to glimpse into my own heart when gazing at it. Pink amethyst is also linked to the womb, helping you to tune into the wisdom and creative energies of your womb space, drawing new love to you. It is a deeply healing crystal that will enable you to trust and believe in love and allow it into your life and heart once more.

Citrine

If you want to have some fun and explore the dating scene, try wearing citrine to help let your inner light and beauty shine out into the world with confidence. You'll be sure to turn heads.

Tiger's eye and malachite

Tiger's eye is good for boldness and bravery and putting yourself out there in the dating world, while malachite will help you to show up as your authentic self and love yourself enough to know what you deserve, so that you can see immediate red flags.

Jade

Wonderful for attracting love into your life and also friendships, jade is a protective crystal that supports you not only in finding new love, but also in gently opening your heart in preparation, allowing you to become aware of any ways in which you are blocking love from coming in.

Kunzite

Kunzite is a crystal of divine love and holds a loving high vibration for connecting you to the love that is always surrounding you. Love is almost certainly on its way to you when you work with kunzite, as this crystal helps you to awaken your heart, trust in love and to freely express your feelings when it comes to matters of the heart.

Rhodochrosite

This is one of the best crystals for attracting love, and especially for calling in those relationships you need to help teach you important and valuable lessons about love in this lifetime – those soulmate relationships. Rhodochrosite will work to open your heart to possibilities and opportunities in love, and also bring out your flirty and playful side, giving you the confidence to be seen. A must-have for all the singles out there.

Twin quartz

If it is deep, soulmate love that you are yearning for, get a twin quartz. This is a pair of crystals of similar size that grow side by side from the same base (with separate points). As the name suggests, this crystal will help to draw your soulmate to you.

Other crystals for welcoming in love: Larimar, rhodonite, rose quartz or pink topaz.

◆ Deepening Existing Love ◆

Once you've found love, crystals can help you to deepen your connection, encourage loyalty and honesty, open your communication and take your love and romance to ever deeper levels.

Emerald

Often called the crystal of successful love, this is a go-to crystal for faith, loyalty and unity. Helping to bring partners closer together and create a deep love connection, it is wonderful to use in the beginning of a new relationship or when you feel that you want to deepen the connection in an existing one.

Rose quartz

With its loving energy, rose quartz in your bedroom will raise the love vibrations. Place rose quartz by the bedside, or you can 'grid' your bed for love by placing a piece at each corner of the bed or underneath it to keep your love and lovemaking sacred and intimate. Rose quartz can also strengthen communication and trust between partners.

Rhodonite

To overcome any difficulties in your relationship, try working with rhodonite. Sometimes referred to as the rescue stone, it is known for its emotional healing. Rhodonite works with your heart, so that you can see your partner with love, bringing acceptance, forgiveness, compassion and open, honest communication. Meditate with a piece of rhodonite in your hand or over your heart and ask for the crystal's assistance in overcoming issues and resolving problems with love. You may also hold your rhodonite when in conversation with your partner so that you speak from your heart (rather than reacting from your mind), communicating from a place of love.

Sugilite

Try working with the 'premier love stone' sugilite to deepen your bond with your partner, while allowing you both the freedom to be yourselves. It supports and deepens love and commitment through good times and bad, helping you to grow through the experiences together. It encourages loving communication and deep, true love.

Garnet, red jasper and carnelian

If you want to invite more sexual intimacy into your relationship, keep pieces of the following in the bedroom or as part of a grid around your bed, too: garnet can bring the desire, passion and spark back, while red jasper or carnelian will reignite the flames of passion and help to recharge the sacral chakra, increasing sexual desire.

Other crystals for deepening existing love: Chrysoprase, amazonite, lapis lazuli or ruby.

CHAPTER 8:

Crystals for . . . Stress and Anxiety

Crystals can be wonderful companions in times when you find yourself overwhelmed, stressed or anxious. Simply holding your chosen crystal and taking ten slow, deep, mindful breaths can often be enough to bring you back into the present moment.

If you find yourself mentally stressed and over-whelmed, work with indigo/dark blue crystals, placing them on your third-eye chakra. If it's your emotions that need some calming, orange crystals over your sacral chakra should do the job. You may also want to include red or grounding crystals on your root chakra to help you ground in times of stress and uncertainty.

Take a look at the calming crystals below and the ways in which you can use them to bring peace of mind, to soothe and balance your frazzled nerves and to bring you calm in times of chaos.

◆ Calming the Mind ◆

Crystals can offer incredible support for those times when you find yourself trapped in your mind, over-thinking, questioning everything or not able to make sense of the jumble of thoughts in your head.

Sodalite

This is one of the first crystals I will always suggest in stressful times of need. Often referred to as the crystal of peace, it helps to calm the mind and is especially useful when you find your thoughts spiralling out of control and you can't make sense of anything. One of the best ways to use sodalite is to carry a piece around with you and hold it in moments when you begin to feel anxious. It's like holding hands with a good friend, and you'll immediately feel its comforting, calming support.

If you know that you are going into a situation or environment that makes you anxious, meditate beforehand holding a piece of sodalite in one hand and focus on your breath as you imagine drawing the calming energies of the crystal in through your hand, up through your arm and into your mind. Feel as though your mind becomes filled with calming, peaceful vibes. You can then send these vibes down into your heart and through your whole body, until your entire being feels calm, peaceful and relaxed. Imagine yourself surrounded by a bubble of peaceful protection.

Fluorite

If you find yourself constantly overthinking every situation or decision, to the point where you end up doing nothing, fluorite is for you. Often called the genius stone, fluorite is great for organising and structuring your thoughts, thinking more clearly and making decisions, especially when under pressure. Try combining it with journaling or a brain dump (where you spill all the contents of your mind out on to paper). Hold a piece of fluorite while writing everything down or when looking back over what you have written, and you may just find its energies will help you to see things much more clearly.

Other crystals for calming the mind: Blue calcite, amethyst, lepidolite or celestite.

Note: at times when you feel your mind is in anxious overdrive, try lying down and placing one of the above crystals on your third-eye area. Lie there for as long as you need to, feeling the energies of the crystal soaking into your mind, bringing calming, soothing, peaceful vibes. Try exhaling out of your mouth, visualising the exhale and crystal working together to release uncertainty, anxiety and the jumble of thoughts in your mind.

◆ Releasing Stuck Thought Patterns ◆

If you find yourself constantly ruminating over the same past events or worrying over an imagined future, stuck in negative thought patterns, crystals can help.

Amethyst

I would suggest using amethyst as a first choice, as it helps release negative thoughts from the mind. If you can use an amethyst point or pyramid, it will be even more powerful. Either sitting or lying down, place your amethyst over your third eye with the point facing away from you. Close your eyes, breathe deeply and visualise the crystal drawing all unwanted and negative thoughts out of your mind. See them floating up into the universe where they will be transmuted and transformed into sparkly new energy.

Other crystals for releasing stuck thought patterns:
A clear quartz point, black tourmaline or kyanite.

◆ Soothing the Emotions ◆

In times of emotional turmoil or when you are caught
in a worry or fear spiral, crystals can help you to
acknowledge, accept, process and heal your emotions,
bringing you inner calm and peace.

Moonstone

Moonstone is wonderful if your emotions are spiralling
out of control. With its feminine, nurturing energies,
moonstone works to balance and calm the emotions. In
particular, if you often find yourself emotionally overre-
acting or not being able to make sense of your emotions,
moonstone will help you to process and heal them, rather
than repressing or supressing them to the point that
they become explosive. Moonstone is particularly useful
for balancing hormones and for those times of the month
when emotions seem to become overwhelming.

Carry moonstone with you and hold it whenever you
feel your emotions rising. You can also meditate with it,
either holding it in your hands or placing a piece over
your heart and/or sacral chakra, allowing the calming
effects to soak into your emotional body. As you meditate,

try inhaling slowly through the nose, as deeply as you can, pausing for a moment and then taking a long, slow, deep exhale out of the mouth, visualising the release of pent-up emotions. You may even add sounds – like a deep sigh, hiss or blowing out of your mouth – to consciously breathe out anger, frustration, sadness or any other overwhelming emotions you may be feeling. Place a couple of quartz points pointing away from you around your body to bring a deep, emotional cleanse at times when you feel really emotionally overwhelmed.

Amazonite

Amazonite is another must-have crystal for your emotions, helping to soothe them in times of emotional turmoil or when all you can feel is worry or fear. This calming crystal brings a sense of balance and peace, helping you to flow with your emotions rather than fight with them.

Kunzite

This beautiful pink crystal is a powerful emotional healer. Kunzite will wrap you in a nurturing, calming and loving energy, soothing your head and heart, especially in the heat of the moment or when emotions feel out of control or overwhelming.

Other crystals for soothing the emotions: Morganite, rose quartz, amethyst or howlite.

◆ Releasing Deeply Held Emotions ◆

Very often, we supress, deny or don't deal with emotions and they become deeply held within us. This is when emotional outbursts or uncontrollable reactions happen, or when we tend to find ourselves stuck in the same emotional patterns over and over again. Working with crystals can help you to uncover and release these deep emotional attachments.

Kyanite blades

If you find that you are carrying around a lot of anger or other intense emotions that you can't seem to let go of, try working with kyanite blades. The blade helps to cut through anger, frustration and stress and to remove emotional hooks and attachments. Often, we continue to be sucked into emotions about a certain situation, person or event as we are still energetically attached to it, which keeps replaying the emotions within us.

Lie down with your arms and legs stretched out as much as is comfortable for you. Take six blue or black kyanite blades (or a mix) and place them around your body: one at the crown of your head, one by your feet

81

and one at each elbow and knee. Lying down with your eyes closed, allow yourself to be drawn to wherever in your body you feel the intensity of the emotion you are feeling and/or any energetic attachments. This may be felt as an intense sensation of the emotion itself, a little tingle, warmth or just that you are more aware of this part of your body. As you focus, visualise any energetic and emotional attachments releasing themselves from your body. Feel the power and energy of the kyanite blades drawing them away. You may even see them float off into space or back to wherever they came from.

You may also add crystals to your third eye (see 'Calming the Mind', p. 78) if your thoughts have also been in emotional overdrive, or to your heart (see 'Healing from Love', p. 65) and/or sacral chakra (see above suggestions) to help with further releasing deep emotion.

Other crystals for releasing deeply held emotions: Malachite, kunzite, apache tears or smoky quartz.

Note: see also Chapter 9 ('Crystals for . . . Energy Clearing and Protection') for information on how to cleanse your energy daily with crystals to keep you free from emotional and energetic cords and attachments.

◆ Grounding on the Earth ◆

A powerful way to manage any emotions, stress and anxiety is to connect to the support, safety and grounding of the earth and release back to it any overwhelming thoughts and feelings to be healed and transmuted.

To do this, stand with one of the crystals mentioned below in each hand. If you can use a smoky quartz point with the point facing down towards the earth, so much the better, but any grounding crystal will do. Now, close your eyes if that feels good, and take a moment to feel your feet on the earth and notice how you feel. Take a long, slow, deep inhale and, as you exhale, imagine any overwhelming thoughts, emotions, concerns, worries, fears, etc. draining out of your mind, down through your heart, belly, body, and legs and out through the soles of your feet down into the earth beneath you. Continue for as long as you need to – until a feeling of calm comes over you – letting go of anything unwanted. You can also do this seated, but make sure that your feet are on the earth.

Alternatively, create a grounding healing grid by making a circle of any of the crystals mentioned below. Once again, you can use smoky quartz points, if you have any, with the points facing away from you to draw off emotion, anxiety and worry. Once you have finished setting up your grid, sit in the centre of the circle of crystals, holding a grounding crystal in each hand. Close your eyes and, as you stay there and breathe deeply and calmly, feel as though these crystals are lovingly absorbing all your emotions, worries, cares, concerns, stress and anxiety and releasing them into the earth. Feel these crystals creating a defensive barrier around you, shielding you from any unwanted energies. Feel grounded and protected in this safe space.

You can also wear or carry your grounding crystals with you, using them as a touchstone to remind you of the earth's support in times of overwhelm. Or meditate with them daily to help keep you connected to the earth and release unwanted energies, emotions, worries or stress.

Smoky quartz

Smoky quartz is one of the best crystals for helping to release negative energy, stress and anxiety. With its cleansing and detoxing properties, it will encourage you to release mental, emotional and energetic baggage and anything unwanted that you no longer need, gently absorbing them from you. It's a powerfully grounding and protective crystal that anchors you to the earth and provides a sense of stability.

Hematite

One of the best crystals to use at times when life feels chaotic and uncertain and you feel unsettled and over-whelmed, hematite will strengthen your connection to the earth, helping you to build a strong foundation within yourself and making you feel grounded, centred and safe. Hematite will work to protect you, drawing away any unwanted energy and feelings of worry or anxiety.

Other crystals for grounding on the earth: Black tourmaline, red jasper, fire agate or obsidian.

◆ Keeping Your Environment ◆ Calm and Peaceful

Crystals in your environment can be great for soothing the mind, emotions and nervous system – absorbing any negative energies, while sending out positive vibes, so that you feel at once more relaxed and at ease.

Apophyllite

I always have a piece of apophyllite in my living space. It is one of the best transmitters of energy and helps to cleanse a room and raise the vibrations to a high frequency.

Clear quartz

Clear quartz clusters are incredibly healing. Known as the master healer, clear quartz will absorb and regulate the energy, radiating positive energy out into your space.

Amethyst and rose quartz

Try an amethyst cluster or chunks of rose quartz to send loving, soothing, calming vibes through the entire room.

Black tourmaline

If you find that you come home from work (or anywhere else) feeling stressed or out of sorts, place a piece of black tourmaline by your front door. Then pause there as you walk in the house and feel the energies of the black tourmaline capture and release any stresses or anxieties you are carrying, leaving your worries at the door. You may visualise this as a shimmery black waterfall at your door that cleanses and washes your day away.

Note: see also see Chapter 11 ('Crystals for . . . Work and Business') for ways to keep your workplace productive and zen and Chapter 9 ('Crystals for . . . Energy Clearing and Protection') for protecting your home.

Other crystals for keeping your environment calm and peaceful: selenite, celestite, citrine or smoky quartz.

> ### *Worry crystals/stones*
> The origins of these have been traced back to ancient Greece, but they have recently made a comeback and have been termed 'pocket tranquillisers'. They are smooth crystals that have either been shaped or naturally have a thumb-sized indentation in them. Holding the crystal between your first two fingers and thumb, you place your thumb in the indentation and gently rub it across the crystal to calm and clear your mind and ease stress and anxiety.
>
> Keep your worry crystal in your pocket and use it as a physical touchstone any time you need it to remind you to take long, slow, deep breaths and be in the present moment, seeking the support you need from it. Choose your touchstone based on what you most need it for – for example: amethyst is a first choice for anxiety and soothing the mind; rose quartz when you want to be surrounded by a loving presence; or tiger's eye for grounding and calming.
>
> I often find that when I am choosing crystals, I pick them for how they feel as I hold them in my hands. I usually naturally find that it's where my thumb fits on the crystal that matters most.

◆ Self-care in Stressful Times ◆

A final reminder here that in times of stress and anxiety we tend to forget all about taking care of ourselves and, as this happens, the feelings of anxiety, stress and overwhelm get worse. In any times of overwhelm, keep some rose quartz nearby to remind you to love and take care of yourself. In times of anxiety, place rose quartz over your heart and take some long, slow, deep breaths to remind you to nurture and care and have compassion for yourself as you work through any difficult thoughts or emotions.

CHAPTER 9:

Crystals for . . .
Energy Clearing and Protection

As we move around through day-to-day life our energies can get out of balance, making us feel disconnected, out of alignment and even down, unmotivated and overly emotional.

When our own energy isn't balanced and protected, we are more likely to leak it and/or take on that of our environments and other people – which is why you can often feel out of sorts or drained after time with certain people or in certain places.

Have a look through all the ways below that you can keep your energy clear and your vibes high. I have also included in this section some crystals that work to protect your home and keep you protected when travelling.

◆ Clear Your Energy ◆

The crystals below will help you to clear your aura and chakras of any trapped or stuck energy or emotions, remove any energetic cords and release anything you are carrying that isn't yours.

Selenite

Using a selenite wand daily will help you to cleanse your aura and remove any energetic or emotional attachments that you have picked up, keeping you balanced, grounded and protected. I usually do this at the end of each day, as though I am clearing the day out of my energy field:

❧ Stand with your feet hip-distance apart, so that you feel deeply rooted and grounded.

❧ Holding your selenite in one hand, close your eyes and take a few long, slow, deep breaths, just feeling into how your energy feels at the end of the day (or whenever you feel out of sorts).

❧ Beginning at the crown of your head, 'comb' the selenite through your energy field, all around the front, back and sides of your body, as though you are brushing your aura clean.

❖ Visualise removing any unwanted energy or emotion, as well as any attachments or cords that have been created through the day.

❖ When you have finished, you can move the selenite down the front of your body, from your crown to your root chakra, to cleanse all your chakras.

Clear quartz

This is another perfect crystal for clearing your energies of any clutter. It will help to absorb and release any unwanted energy, aligning your chakras and energy bodies and bringing your whole being – body, mind, heart and soul – back into a state of balance. Hold a piece of clear quartz (or any of the crystals mentioned below) as you take long, slow, deep breaths, visualising each exhale carrying away anything unwanted in your energy. You can also place clear quartz points around your body, with the points facing away to draw off any stuck or trapped energies.

Other crystals for clearing your energy: amethyst, fluorite, kyanite or black tourmaline.

Note: see also Chapter 6 ('Crystals for . . . the Chakras') for clearing and balancing your chakras.

◆ Protect Your Energy ◆

Once you've cleared your own energy field, you may want to keep it protected, especially when spending time with certain people or heading into situations and environments that can drain you.

Carry any of the crystals mentioned below with you for protection. Or you can use them in an energy grid that you sit or stand inside on days when you know you are going to need some extra protection: placing the crystals in a circle, sit or stand inside the grid, stay here, or even meditate here for 5 to 10 minutes, feeling the crystals create an energetic field that surrounds and protects you.

Black tourmaline

My go-to for protecting my energy is black tourmaline. Wear this crystal when you are out and about or heading into draining situations to create a shield of protection around you that nothing can penetrate. If my energy feels off at any time, I touch the tourmaline to strengthen the protection and deflect any unwanted energy coming my way.

Fire agate

Another amazing crystal for building a protective shield around you and deflecting any unwanted energies, fire agate is particularly powerful if you ever have to head into situations of conflict or when you feel that people are sending unwarranted judgement or criticism your way. Fire agate helps to return any harm to its original source so that the person responsible can learn from it. Wear or hold your crystal and imagine a shield around your energy. You can also place it by the windows of your home if you have issues with neighbours.

Jet

If you find that you often take on other people's moods or energies, jet will act as an energetic filter, working to keep these out of your aura.

Labradorite

Labradorite is powerful for making sure there is a protective boundary between you and other people's emotions and energies. It is especially useful to wear or have with you around those people who always want something from you and drain your energy reserves.

Other crystals for protecting your energy: obsidian, jasper, smoky quartz, hematite or amethyst.

◆ Protection for Your Home ◆

Having crystals around your home will help to keep the energy of your home cleansed and protected. Crystals can also make excellent security guards to help ensure your home is a safe haven.

Selenite

I always have a selenite tower in my home to clear and protect the energy of where I live. Selenite helps to absorb negative emotions and energy and cleanses the environment. Try gridding your room or home with a selenite tower in each corner to create a protective energetic shield around your living space.

Black tourmaline

You can further protect the energy of your home by placing black tourmaline either with your selenite or by itself by your front door. Similar to asking people to take off their shoes to keep your house clean, black tourmaline will work to draw off any negative energy as people enter your space.

Note: you may also try placing crystals by your Wi-Fi router, TV, computers and other electronic devices to help shield you and your home from EMF (electromagnetic fields). I have always kept a piece of black tourmaline next to my TV, selenite by my computer and shungite on top of my Wi-Fi router.

Other crystals for protecting your home: rose quartz, citrine, apophyllite or clear quartz.

◆ Protection for Travel ◆

Crystals make perfect travel companions to help keep you protected, stress-free and calm and relaxed on your journey.

Black kyanite and black tourmaline
I always keep a piece of black kyanite in my car to protect me and keep me safe on the road. You can use black tourmaline, too, which is also powerful for deflecting any road rage sent your way.

Moonstone and amethyst
Moonstone has long been known as the traveller's stone and so is one of your best companions on your travels.

Carry a piece with you at all times to ensure a smooth journey and protection on your travels, especially when travelling over water. It will also help you to overcome symptoms of jetlag more quickly and easily.

If travelling makes you anxious, take amethyst with you to soothe and calm your nerves. A highly protective crystal, amethyst will wrap you in a loving bubble of protection on your journey, working to alleviate travel sickness.

Both moonstone and amethyst will help not only to protect you, but also your luggage, so make sure you pack a piece, too.

Malachite

Malachite is often gifted to airline workers as a talisman to protect them when flying. If you're scared of flying, hold a piece of malachite throughout the journey, or especially at take-off and landing, to keep your fears and anxieties at bay and protect you during the flight.

Other crystals for protection for travel: tiger's eye, rose quartz, smoky quartz or clear quartz.

CHAPTER 10:

Crystals for . . .
Manifesting and Abundance

When it comes to manifesting and abundance, crystals are your go-to support squad for supercharging your wishes and bringing abundance in all areas of your life.

Yellow crystals over your solar-plexus chakra can be helpful in lighting up your personal power and making you magnetic to all you wish to manifest. A crystal pyramid is a wonderful choice for manifesting, as the point beams your intentions out into the world, while the base anchors them in reality.

◆ Manifest Your Desires ◆

The crystals below will work with you to make you magnetic to all that you desire and to beam your intentions out into the world, bringing them more easily to life.

Clear quartz

One of your first choices for manifesting should be clear quartz, which, as the master crystal, can be used to manifest anything and everything. Clear quartz amplifies the energy of any intention, dream or wish that is programmed into it and will continue to draw your desires to you, even when you are not consciously thinking about it.

Clear quartz can also bring clarity to your mind and heart, and therefore your intentions. If you are not certain about the direction of your life or what your dreams or desires are, try meditating with a piece of clear quartz for a few weeks to allow any blockages to be removed and to get crystal clear on your intentions.

Once you have decided what it is that you want to manifest, take some time to connect with your clear quartz and set your intentions. Tell the crystal what you would like it to help you to manifest. Be as clear and specific as you can (you may want to look back at Chapter 4 for more information about how to set intentions with your crystals).

Once you have set your intention on your clear quartz, either carry it around with you or spend some time each day holding it and visualising your life as though your dream has already come true; the more energy and power you can give to your intentions, the more quickly they can manifest into your life.

Clear quartz points and towers can be extremely powerful when sending your intentions out into the world and drawing to you what you desire. Try writing your intentions down and placing them under a clear quartz tower, where it will beam them out into the universe for you. Or place quartz points around your intention-charged clear quartz with the points facing in to draw even more power to your manifestations. Clear quartz points can be placed around any crystal or grid or any of the crystals below that you have set intentions on to bring even more power, energy and magic to your desires. You can even try placing clear quartz points in a circle around yourself with the points facing towards you as you meditate on your intentions and desires, visualising them coming true. The quartz points will help draw towards you all that you need to make your dream a reality.

Manifestation quartz

A small crystal encased in a larger crystal, these – as the name suggests – are incredibly powerful for mani-festing your dreams. They are quite rare, and so slightly harder to come by, but if you have a big dream or desire you want to manifest, keep a look out for this one. Set your intentions on one of these and then meditate holding it each day and watch your dreams come true.

Citrine

Your solar-plexus chakra is your place of personal power from where you magnetise yourself to your dreams and desires, drawing them towards you. Place a piece of citrine over your solar-plexus chakra and spend five to ten minutes breathing into this place of power and allowing the energies of the citrine to supercharge you. Feel the abundance, the manifestation, the magnetism, as though you are easily attracting to yourself all that you desire. You can even add some clear quartz or citrine points around your body, points facing towards you, turning yourself into an even bigger magnet for your dreams and desires.

If there is something big that I want to manifest into my life, I meditate holding a citrine point facing towards me to draw to me all that I desire. You can also hold a citrine point and clear quartz point (or any of the crystals below that resonate with what you want to manifest), while repeating affirmations around your intentions and desires. Either create an affirmation specific to your intention ('I easily and effortlessly manifest my business ideas into reality', for example) or a more generic one ('Everything I desire is coming to me now').

Other crystals for manifesting your desires: rose quartz (for manifesting love), pyrite (for manifesting wealth), blue apatite (for manifesting your ideas into reality), green aventurine (for manifesting new opportunities) and amethyst (for manifesting wisdom and self-awareness).

◆ Opening to Abundance ◆

Work with the magical crystals below to help open you up to receiving the very best that life has to offer; it's time to welcome in the prosperity, joy and happiness that you deserve.

Citrine

Citrine is my abundance crystal of choice. This beautiful little ray of golden sunshine has a vibrant energy and has been dubbed the merchant's stone for the prosperity it attracts.

I always keep a piece of citrine in my purse to attract more money and wealth; you can do the same with a wallet or cash register or anywhere you keep money, to ensure a flow of financial abundance.

I also have a grid of citrine and pyrite in the wealth

corner of my house (this is the farthest left corner of your house or any room as you stand with your back to the door). I write out affirmations of abundance such as 'Money comes to me easily and effortlessly' or 'I am magnetic to money, prosperity and abundance' and place the citrine and pyrite over these affirmations to keep drawing more wealth and abundance into my life. You can also place citrine over notes of money or even write yourself an imaginary cheque for however much you want to attract into your life and let citrine help you to open the flow of abundance.

Remember that abundance isn't just about money. It's joy, happiness, laughter, adventure, connection – it's about being open to and receiving all the good things that the universe has to offer you.

Sunstone

As the name suggests, this beautiful little crystal is filled with the energies of the sun, bringing light, life, energy and joy. If life has lost some of its sparkle, meditate with, wear or carry around a piece of sunstone to help you to see the light. Sunstone is also incredible when it comes to shining your light out into the world.

Amazonite

This brings a playful, childlike energy, encouraging you to let go of all you are trying to control and go with the flow of life. You'll feel hope and optimism and a sense of being open to whatever life has to offer when amazonite is around.

Clear quartz

This is great for reminding you that you are part of something way greater. It will connect you to the universe, your higher self, intuition and guides (see p. 152), helping you to feel expansive and connected to the abundant flow of life and the guidance and wisdom that surround you at all times.

Other crystals for opening to abundance: rose quartz, labradorite, malachite or apophyllite.

◆ Removing Blocks to ◆ Manifesting and Abundance

Manifesting and abundance are a state of mind and it all starts with feeling good about and believing in yourself. You have to believe that you truly deserve to have abundance and prosperity, otherwise you subconsciously refuse and block it. If you find yourself blocked from being able to manifest what you want into your life, try working with the crystals below.

Tiger's eye

This will bring you a confidence boost and a reminder of how powerful and capable you are. It will give you the courage to go after what you truly want.

Chrysocolla

This will remind you of your personal power and bring a hit of motivation to make changes in your life.

Carnelian

As well as helping to raise your sense of self-worth and boost your confidence, carnelian also brings the courage to follow opportunities.

Other crystals for removing blocks to manifesting and abundance: hematite, lapis lazuli, black tourmaline or amethyst.

Note: you may also want to look back over the self-love section (p. 62), how to cleanse your chakras (p. 58) or how to clear and protect your energy (pp. 90–3).

CHAPTER 11:

Crystals for . . .
Work and Business

Whether you're at the interview stage, dreaming of setting up on your own or wanting to expand in your career or company, crystals can make the perfect business partners. They can also work with office environments and protecting your energy.

◆ Attracting the Right Job, ◆
Career and Clients

Call on the assistance of these hard-working crystals when you want to expand in your career and make yourself seen and heard.

Citrine

When it comes to career success, citrine will act as your own personal recruitment agency. Take some time to get very clear on what you want from your work or job. What would you be doing each day? How would it feel? How would you contribute and make a difference? If you know the exact career path that you want to take, get as specific as you can and go into as much detail about it as possible. Write it all down and place it underneath a citrine tower, so that the crystal can beam your energetic CV out into the world, working to attract the perfect job for you. You can surround this with citrine (or clear quartz) points facing in to help draw this into your life more quickly.

The same thing can also be done in existing businesses where you want to attract more interest. Take your business card or write down details of ways in which you want to develop your business and place citrine, pyrite and rose quartz on top to bring more business your way. If you want to attract a certain number of new clients, get specific on how many you want. Spend some time meditating with your citrine, letting it know these things. Meditate holding your crystal every day and visualise its bright golden energy coming in through your hands and filling your body. Imagine every cell in your body infused with this golden light and your intention to attract your new clients and business; feel the desire in every part of you. Feel as it fills you up and starts to surround and beam out of you, as though you are an energetic lighthouse, calling and attracting your clients. Imagine them easily seeing and following your bright light to find their way to you. Beam your business out into the world.

Chrysoprase

Hold a piece of chrysoprase when completing application forms or business paperwork. This supportive crystal will help you to believe in your talents and abilities, giving you the confidence and courage that you have what it takes.

Pyrite

This will encourage you to believe in yourself and what you have to offer and to know your value and worth in your career and business. It's a great crystal to hold or meditate with in moments of doubt and when you don't feel worthy of work or success. It will enhance your willpower, boost your confidence and inspire you to get things done.

Aventurine

If you need a lucky break, try meditating with aventurine to open you up to new opportunities in your career and business. This crystal will help you to overcome any doubts or fears and shift your perspective to one of hopeful optimism, enabling you to create your own luck and attract the right job or clients to you.

Other crystals for attracting the right job, career and clients: sunstone, jade, rose quartz or malachite.

◆ Acing the Interview Process ◆

Set an intention on any of the crystals below to help you breeze through the interview process. Meditate with your chosen crystal on the morning of the interview and then keep it close at hand, either by wearing it or keeping it in a pocket throughout. After the interview, while you are waiting for the decision, you can place your crystal inside a grid of clear quartz to keep empowering the process and meditate with it daily, visualising getting the job.

Tiger's eye
If it's a boost of bravery and courage that you need, look no further than tiger's eye. Wear this crystal, hold it or keep it in your pocket or close by during interviews to ensure that you remain grounded, bold and brave throughout. Working with the solar-plexus chakra, tiger's eye will ensure that you allow the very best of you to shine, bringing out the most confident and empowered version of you.

Sodalite

Sodalite will not only help to calm your nerves, but also to communicate effectively. As it brings peace and clarity to your mind, it will work to organise your thoughts and help you to speak clearly and confidently when answering questions. As it also encourages you to access your intuitive mind, it is great for bypassing nerves and the monkey mind and accessing your deeper wisdom. Wear or hold throughout, perhaps even taking a moment to hold it to your third eye and throat right before the interview to infuse you with its vibes.

Rose quartz

Rose quartz is an excellent interview crystal as it will keep you connected to your heart and keep reminding you of your value and worth and what you can bring to the position.

Other crystals for acing the interview process: lapis lazuli, labradorite, aventurine or blue lace agate.

◆ Support for Your First Day ◆ at Work or New Business Venture

Crystals can offer you so much support when you are stepping into the new and unknown. Keep your chosen crystals with you at all times as you enter new territories, either by wearing or holding them in times of need.

Malachite

Malachite is often one of my first choices for any kind of new beginning. As the crystal of transformation, it helps you to embrace change and adapt to the new. Its protective energy will be like having a supportive friend by your side, encouraging you on. It works to overcome shyness and nerves and connects you to your heart, allowing your true self to shine through.

Chrysocolla

If you're just starting out on a new job, project or business endeavour, use chrysocolla to bring not only motivation and excitement, but also fresh, new energy, propelling you confidently into change and connecting you to the venture from your heart, drawing to you the people, support and connections that you need to make it a success.

Carnelian

Carnelian will bring the bravery you need to face big, new projects or ventures. Associated with passion and creativity, it is particularly powerful in helping you to get passion projects off the ground. Known as the stone for new opportunities, it will support you in achieving your goals and staying motivated, inspired and creative throughout the process.

Other crystals for your first day at work or new business venture: tigers' eye, green aventurine, jade or moonstone.

◆ Continuing Your Career Success ◆

If you are looking to climb the corporate ladder or expand in your business, these crystals are for you. Work with them close by, placing them in a grid over a business plan or holding them as you repeat affirmations out loud, such as 'I deserve success'.

Sunstone

A go-to for promotion, new opportunities or allowing yourself to expand and shine in your business or career. Meditate daily with sunstone, either over your solar-plexus chakra or in your hands, to feel your inner strength, power and self-belief expand. Sunstone will help you to express yourself, to be seen and heard, to stand in your power and to achieve all that you know you are capable of.

Jade

Jade will help you to achieve your career goals, overcoming any limitations and guiding you to make the right decisions. A crystal of luck and prosperity, keep it close by for formulating long-term goals and continuing to earn, grow and achieve in your business.

Amazonite

Known as the stone of success or of hope, amazonite supports you in getting confidently clear on not only where you want to go, but also how to get there. Working with your heart chakra, it will assist you in believing and trusting in yourself and nudge you to get out of your comfort zone to go after what your heart truly desires.

Other crystals for career success: carnelian, fluorite, tiger's eye or rose quartz.

◆ Keeping Your Workplace ◆ Productive and Zen

Having crystals around you at work can help to raise the energy and vibration of your workplace, provide protection from colleagues, clients and bosses and keep you feeling calm and in control.

Smoky quartz and black tourmaline

If you find your work environment stressful, try keeping a piece of smoky quartz or black tourmaline on your desk to shield you against negative energies and colleagues or even bosses!

Clear quartz and amethyst

A clear quartz cluster in your workspace will work to filter out any negative energies and fill the area with positive vibrations. Amethyst is also a good option for raising your workplace vibrations to a calm, peaceful, loving energy and for finding balance in your mind and emotions in times of stress.

Other crystals for keeping your workplace productive and zen: selenite to cleanse away tense emotions or energies from difficult customers or colleagues; hematite, to absorb draining energies and emotions; rose quartz for remaining in your heart and treating people with compassion and empathy; labradorite to prevent you from absorbing and taking on other people's negative or angry energies; blue lace agate for calm and clear communication.

Note: crystals can also offer powerful protection from technology and EMF (electromagnetic fields). Place a piece of shungite, hematite, pyrite or black tourmaline near your computer to help counteract the negative effects of some of your screen time.

CHAPTER 12:

Crystals for . . . Finding Your Power and Moving Forward

When you need to find and stand in your power, speak your truth and find the courage to set boundaries or let go and move on in your life, crystals are your cheer-leading squad.

◆ Standing in Your Power ◆

Standing in your power means knowing who you are and what you are capable of, trusting in yourself, following your dreams and being responsible for your own happiness.

When you are deeply rooted in your own power, nothing and nobody can shake the foundation of who you are. But let's face it: it can be way too easy to give your power away, whether to other people or to your own self-doubt and self-sabotage – especially if this is something you have spent most of your life doing. This is where crystals can be a big support.

Crystals for your solar-plexus and root chakras

Your solar plexus is your place of personal power and so wearing or meditating with crystals such as citrine, sunstone, tiger's eye or carnelian placed here will help you to replenish, strengthen and maintain your source of power.

We also want to be grounded and rooted in our power, so don't forget your root chakra, especially if you struggle to stay in your power for more than fleeting moments. Try meditating with or carrying black tourmaline, smoky quartz, red jasper or bloodstone. Meditate with, carry or simply hold any of the crystals below when you need a crystal-powered boost of energy.

Labradorite

Labradorite is quite simply a magical crystal to work with when stepping into your inner power as that's just what it will support you in doing: believe in your own magic. This stunning crystal will help to reflect back to you the light and power within you, giving you the power and courage to believe in yourself and what you have to offer and allowing you to know and own yourself, so that you are not afraid to show up in the world as you.

Malachite

Malachite will help you to protect and guard your inner power, so make sure that you wear or carry it when you are going into situations that you know test your resolve.

Fire opal

As its name suggests, this crystal brings a fiery energy to light up your inner personal power and keep it ablaze, protecting you against anything that tries to dim it.

Black obsidian

At times when self-doubt is keeping you powerless, obsidian will reflect your inner strength and power back to you, helping you to connect to and know who you are and what you are capable of.

Larimar

When you need to step up and take back power and control over your life, larimar will help you to see and release any self-sabotaging behaviour and limiting beliefs that you use – or allow – to hold yourself back.

Other crystals for standing in your power: charoite, moldavite, black onyx or peridot.

> **Note:** see also Chapter 15 ('Crystals for . . . Connecting to a Higher Power'), as this will help you to strengthen and trust in your inner knowing.

◆ Creating Healthy Boundaries ◆

If you find yourself constantly giving your power away, struggling with setting boundaries and always saying yes when you mean no, these crystals can awaken your inner power.

Sunstone

Sunstone will help you to say no when you mean no and overcome any feelings of fear that come with this. It is also one of the best crystals for awakening your inner power. Place a piece of sunstone over your solar-plexus chakra and visualise the bright yellow inner sunshine of that chakra becoming clearer and stronger as it soaks up the power of the sunstone. As you lie there, imagine that with each exhale you release any guilt or fear of dark clouds of expectation from others that are hanging around you. Once you have done this, and are hopefully already feeling lighter and brighter, begin to fill your body with this sunshine energy, feeling it activate the power and bravery within you to say no.

Feel it filling your aura and creating a healthy boundary around you. Say to yourself 'I have the power to say no; it is safe for me to say no' as many times as you need to, until you feel the force and the truth of these words in your body. Alternatively, try 'I fearlessly activate all of my power', if you want to remind yourself of the power within you.

Amazonite

Use amazonite to set boundaries based on the needs of your own heart and what is best for you, as well as for sticking to them and staying true to yourself and your decisions, releasing any fear of judgement. Keep this crystal close by when you need to affirm, reiterate or strengthen your boundaries or when they are being questioned or pushed by others. Amazonite will also support you in communicating your boundaries from a clear and firm yet loving and compassionate place.

Other crystals for creating healthy boundaries: rose quartz, malachite, chrysocolla or tiger's eye.

◆ Speaking Your Truth ◆

When you need to speak your truth, use crystals to find and amplify your voice, making yourself heard.

Any blue crystals over your throat chakra will help to clear and balance your voice, so try this before any difficult or deep conversations or when speaking in public. Remember that our words carry such powerful vibrations and meaning, so we want to be as truthful and authentic in our interactions as possible.

Or, to open up your communication channels, try holding one of the crystals below in your receiving hand as you journal and use this as an opportunity to convey anything that needs to be said or heard in that moment. Don't overthink it, just allow the words to flow on to the paper (it can be destroyed afterwards, which often makes it easier for us to be more honest about what we write, as there is no fear around it ever being seen).

Lapis lazuli

Lapis lazuli is one of my go-to crystals when I need to find my voice. Not only does it help to open the throat chakra, this crystal of truth also ensures that your words come from a place of deep authenticity and that you can speak your truth, expressing yourself clearly, openly and honestly, so that you say what you mean and mean what you say. Meditate with lapis over your third eye or throat to tune into your deepest inner truth and hold or wear it at times when you need to communicate this. If you have supressed your voice for a long time, this can feel quite intense and too much to begin with; imagine a hosepipe with a kink in it – you want to let the water out gradually, rather than in one big tsunami. In which case, it may be better to begin with blue lace agate . . .

Blue lace agate

This is a soothing crystal for beginning to gently find your voice and express yourself. If you're afraid to speak up, this crystal will hold you in a loving energy, working to calm your emotions and ease any anxiety as you start to find your voice. Wear blue lace agate (particularly near your throat) to help heal your voice and learn to express yourself with confidence and ease.

Other crystals for speaking your truth: blue kyanite, chrysocolla, amazonite or celestite.

◆ Letting Go ◆

If you are always living in the past or are weighed down by emotional baggage and limiting thoughts or beliefs, it may be time to use the power of crystals to heal and let go.

Black obsidian

This crystal is not only good for dissolving away ties to the past, but also for grounding you in the present and bringing your focus back into the moment. Meditate with or hold obsidian, especially when you find your mind wandering back into the past. Black obsidian is also powerful when trying to release limiting beliefs and unconscious thought patterns that cause you to repeat the same behaviours. Wear obsidian when you find yourself stuck in patterns of limiting beliefs or meditate with it daily to help release their grip on your mind.

Selenite and kyanite

You can use a selenite wand or kyanite blade for 'cutting ties' to the past. Sit in a comfortable position and take a few long, slow, deep breaths. Begin to visualise in your mind's eye the person or situation that you still find yourself energetically connected to. You may take a few moments here to say anything to them about any lessons learned and why it's now time to let go. Feel where in your body there is still a connection to this person or situation; your awareness may be drawn there automatically, or you may notice a tingling or sensation somewhere. Then hold your selenite or kyanite over that place in your body and affirm your readiness and willingness to let go. When you feel that it's time, you can either lovingly cut this cord or my preferred way is to use your crystal to unhook and draw it out of your body and see it float back to where it came from.

You can also use a selenite wand or kyanite blade in a similar way for releasing any limiting thoughts or trapped emotional energy. Take your wand or blade and point it at your third eye to free up your mind – or anywhere in your body you feel that you are holding stuck emotions. Circle the wand or blade a few times over the area and then draw it away from you, as though you are drawing out and releasing away the thoughts, doubts, fears or emotions. I often visualise shaking them off the end of the wand or blade and seeing them being released out into the loving energy of the universe to be dissolved and healed.

Amethyst and rose quartz
If you find that you are weighed down by emotional baggage, use amethyst to release this and move on.

Meditating or journaling with this beautiful, soothing crystal is great for working through any painful experiences and emotions, processing why something happened, learning the lessons and letting go. Try meditating with an amethyst point to draw away and release any emotional or painful attachments that are holding you back. Add rose quartz if there is a lot of guilt or resentment involved and to help you to bring love and compassion for all involved, including yourself.

Chrysocolla

If it's limiting beliefs that keep you stuck, chrysocolla is the crystal for dissolving these and, in their place, developing a sense of self-belief and power in your thoughts. Known as a teaching stone, it will encourage you to gently question your thoughts and whether they are true, opening you up to being curious about new ways of thinking about yourself and your life. Wear chrysocolla to help you break through and beyond the limits of your mind, meditate with it when the resistance from your mind is strong and hold it while repeating positive affirmations, such as: 'I know that I am capable of whatever I put my mind to' or 'I believe in myself'.

Other crystals for letting go: moonstone, smoky quartz, carnelian or citrine.

◆ Creating Change ◆ and Moving Forward

One of the main reasons why we hold on to relationships, beliefs, jobs or other things that we know, deep down, are not good for us is fear: fear of change, or of the unknown. Turn to these crystals to realise what changes need to be made and bring you the bravery to make them and move forward in your life.

Rose quartz
If you know changes need to be made in your life, but you're not sure what or how, start by working with rose quartz. The loving, gentle energy of this crystal will help you to connect to your heart and begin to face your fears with love, encouraging you to believe and trust in yourself enough to know that you can face any challenges and changes and get through them. Work with rose quartz daily to uncover the truth of your heart and what you yearn for in your life, so you know where and how to go about changing things. You could do this through meditation or journaling with your rose quartz.

Jet
Jet is powerful for overcoming fear of change and the unknown. So if fear is keeping you frozen in place and preventing you from making any changes or

decisions, meditate with jet daily to help keep your fears at bay.

Hematite

If you know you need to make changes, but you don't know how, hematite is the way to go. It's a strongly supportive crystal that will not only reassure you that you've got this and it's all going to be ok, but will also guide you forward into the new experiences that are waiting for you. Meditate with or carry it so it can show you the way.

Tiger's eye

Once you're clear on the changes that need to be made, tiger's eye will bring you the courage and bravery to face your fears with strength. Wear or carry it with you and it will encourage and support you in boldly moving forward with any necessary changes.

Smoky quartz

This crystal will also encourage you to bring any required changes into reality, giving them structure and a clear plan of action. Meditate holding smoky quartz or with a point facing towards you to help bring needed change.

Malachite

And finally, if you're really and truly ready to make change, work with the crystal of transformation: malachite. But be warned – it will bring change and bring it fast. Working with malachite often brings about immediate and big changes, pushing you to take action. It's almost as though everything is falling apart, but, in fact, it's coming together. Anything that is not meant for you will be obvious and clear when malachite is involved in a life review. Make a list of all that isn't working in your life and ask for malachite's assistance in bringing about the necessary changes. Wear or carry it with you to help with taking action, or place it in a grid over your life review to bring changes in any required areas.

Other crystals for creating change and moving forward: rhodonite, carnelian, labradorite or clear quartz.

CHAPTER 13:

Crystals for . . .
Moon Magic

As a self-confessed moon child, I had to include a section on how to use crystals with the moon to create a little more moon magic.

Moonstone is the first and most obvious choice to connect with lunar energies. As its name suggests, it is strongly connected to the moon and is one of the best crystals to work with to enhance your moon magic. Selenite is also a good option (named after Selene, the Greek goddess of the moon).

So first, let's look briefly at how we can work with the moon's energies, and then how to use crystals to work even more powerfully with them.

Using the Moon's Energies

Working with the moon has quite simply changed my life. We can learn so much from the moon and her ever-changing cycles, and, in turn, tune into her energies to help us flow with the rhythms and cycles of our own lives. Using the moon's energies to release and let go allows us to create space for new beginnings and amazing opportunities for ourselves, ensuring that we continue to grow and move forward in life, rather than holding ourselves back or staying stuck in the past.

Month by month, moon by moon, working with lunar energies gives us the opportunity to check in with where we are in our lives, and whether that's where we want to be. From there, we get to make conscious change, releasing whatever stands in the way and moving our lives in the direction of our dreams.

The new moon brings the opportunity for new

beginnings and new direction. Use the day of the new moon to identify what you truly want in your life and start to plant the seeds of growth: make wishes, set intentions, dream and imagine all that's possible for you.

During the waxing lunar cycle (when the moon is growing bigger), continue to add energy to the intentions and goals you have set and take any action that you can to help make your dreams a reality.

The full moon is a time of celebrations, endings, completion and letting go. On the day of the full moon, celebrate what you have achieved since the new moon, then use the full-moon energies to identify what stood in the way of you achieving your goals, any areas in which you would like to see change or things you want to release. This can be anything from negative thoughts, grief or anger to relationships or jobs.

Use the period of the waning lunar cycle (when the moon is becoming smaller) to continue letting go of anything that's standing in the way of you manifesting your goals, affirming your willingness to release any obstacles to happiness.

(If you are keen to learn more about moon magic and working with lunar energies, be sure to read my *Sunday Times* bestselling book, *Lunar Living: Working with the magic of the moon cycles*.)

◆ Using Your Moonstone ◆

Moonstone is about new beginnings. It will help you to bring your moon intentions to life, linking you to your intuition and the waxing and waning cycles of the moon.

On a new moon, hold your moonstone and state out loud or whisper in your heart your new-moon intentions for the coming cycle. Ask your moonstone for support, guidance and wisdom in bringing these intentions to life. Then leave your moonstone on your altar or in a special place or grid (see opposite), where it will continue to send out the energetic vibes of your new-moon intentions into the world, helping them to manifest. Once a day through the waxing phase of the lunar cycle, meditate with or hold your moonstone for a few moments, visualising your new-moon wishes and dreams. I often find that during these daily moments of connection with my moonstone, I get intuitive guidance and clarity on things I need to do.

Reconnect with your moonstone on the full moon, meditating with it and looking back over the two weeks since the new moon. What has worked and what hasn't? In what areas did you give the required energy to your new-moon dreams and intentions and where did you get distracted, scared or pulled off track? Use your moonstone now to set your intentions of what you need to release over the waning part of the lunar cycle. Once more, whisper them to your moonstone, asking for help and guidance in releasing whatever stands in the way. Again, place your moonstone on your altar or special place, where it will continue to work with you on releasing and letting go. Once a day over the waning lunar cycle, meditate with or hold your moonstone with the intention of releasing all that you no longer need.

You can also add selenite to this ritual to bring in even more moon magic. Take a look at how to clear your energy on p. 90 and include this moon-time energy cleanse on a new and full moon. Imagine the light of the moon helping you to further cleanse away anything you no longer need.

◆ More Lunar Crystal Magic ◆

Add other crystals to your moonstone to increase the potency of your moon magic. One of the most powerful ways to work with lunar cycles and crystals is to create grids. I begin the grid on the night of the new moon and keep it in place throughout the lunar cycle. I may then refresh it, completely change it or keep it in place for a further lunar cycle if the same intentions need some extra moon magic.

A simple grid is to use clear quartz points around

your moonstone. On a new moon and through the waxing part of the cycle, the points should face in, to keep bringing energy to your new-moon intention. On the full moon and through the waning part of the cycle, the points should be turned out, for releasing and letting go of what no longer serves you. You may include some selenite in this grid to draw in even more lunar energy. And when you are not using or meditating with your moonstone, keep it inside this grid of quartz crystals to keep amplifying your moon intentions.

You can add other crystals to your grid too. Or when you are meditating/visualising daily, hold your moonstone in one hand and another crystal in the other depending on what your new moon intentions are focused around. For example, for love, add rose quartz; for business ventures, citrine; and for being brave and bold, tiger's eye. Black tourmaline is incredible for releasing through the waning part of the lunar cycle, as are kyanite or labradorite. Howlite will support you in setting better boundaries; or try amethyst or labradorite for following your intuition. And take a look through the other chapters of this book for life areas in which you are setting your intentions, adding the relevant crystals for bringing even more power and focus to these and your crystal-moon magic. You can also read up on crystals for the zodiac signs on p. 155 and use crystals relevant to the sign that each new and full moon is in.

Lastly, if you want to wear moonstone as jewellery, it will help with keeping you connected to the energies of the moon and going with the rhythm and flow of life, trusting in what is unfolding for you through the cycle. Just be warned that if you are moon-sensitive, it might feel a bit too much wearing it around a full moon, when the lunar energies peak, so you may need to remove it for these few days.

CHAPTER 14:

Crystals for . . . Sleep and Relaxation

If you have trouble winding down, can't seem to drop off easily to sleep, find yourself in the wide-awake club in the early hours or want to work with your dreams, there is a crystal here to support you.

A Crystal bath

One thing I love to do is take a bath with crystals, and I always turn this into a real act of self-care.

Light some candles, play relaxing music, add some beautiful bath oils and make sure your phone and all tech are out of the room. Choose the crystals you want to work with (always remembering to check that they're not water-soluble) and place them in the running bath water, asking that they help to infuse the water with their vibrational energy for you to absorb.

As you relax in your crystal bath, take long, slow breaths and imagine your crystals drawing all the stresses, worries and anxieties out of your body, while the water cleanses them away. Soak for as long as you need to and when you are done, as you pull the plug, feel all your cares drain away with the water.

Rose quartz

It's rumoured that Cleopatra bathed with chunks of rose quartz, so you may follow her lead and add it for some self-love vibes.

Other crystals for taking a bath

Amethyst (for deep relaxation), clear quartz (for deep cleansing), smoky quartz (for deep healing) or even a crystal for one or each chakra.

◆ A Bedtime Relaxation Routine ◆

An evening routine before bed is great for sleep troubles. This not only lets your mind and body know that the time for sleep is coming, but also encourages you to put aside stresses from your day and create a calm space.

The combined magic of crystals and yoga

One of the best things for deep relaxation before bed is a yoga pose called viparita karani. This deeply restorative pose will help to calm the mind, relieve anxiety and completely relax the entire nervous system. Just add crystals and you're on a one-way street to deep relaxation like never before.

How to do it:

1. Decide which crystals you want to use and have them close by.

2. Sit on the floor with one hip flush against a wall.

3. Gently swing your legs around, until they are up the wall with the backs of your thighs resting against it. Make sure your buttocks are as close to the wall as possible and your arms are down by your sides, palms facing up.

4. Place the relevant crystals on your body. You may even cover yourself with a blanket, too, and put an eye pillow over your eyes, if desired.

5. Stay in this position for 10–15 minutes, before slowly lowering yourself down to lie on your back.

While you are here, you may place sodalite or amethyst on your third eye to bring peace of mind, rose quartz on your heart or moonstone on your sacral chakra to soothe your emotions, and even hold a crystal of your choosing in each hand to feel the connection to the healing energy.

You could even turn this into a proper self-care ritual at any time of day by adding a crystal to each chakra (see Chapter 6 – 'Crystals for . . . the Chakras') or by placing your body inside a crystal grid of choice to help with any stresses or issues you may be facing. Burn some incense, play soothing music and relax deeply, breathing all your troubles away.

Selenite

Another powerful ritual before bed is journaling, to get out all the things that would otherwise run through your mind in the middle of the night, keeping you awake. Hold a piece of selenite while you write, and this powerful crystal will work to cleanse all that troubles you out of your mind, body and heart and on to the paper. You can then use the selenite to cleanse your aura and chakras (see p. 90) for a full pre-bedtime cleansing ritual. Keep your selenite nearby through the night, as it also helps with insomnia.

Other crystals for a bedtime relaxation routine: blue lace agate, lepidolite, pink tourmaline or smoky quartz.

◆ Sleeping Soundly ◆

If you struggle to drop off to sleep or you wake in the middle of the night, crystals can become the perfect bed companion to help you sleep soundly. They can also help you to access, remember and work with your dreams.

Amethyst
Probably one of the first crystals that will be recommended for insomnia and sleep troubles, amethyst has serene, calming and soothing vibes that wrap you in a bubble of peace, ready for a good night's sleep. Keep an amethyst geode on your bedside table or a tumbled piece inside your pillowcase or under your pillow for a great night's sleep. Amethyst also helps with nightmares, so if you suffer from these, be sure to have a

piece nearby, so that it can protect you while you are sleeping.

Howlite

Speaking of dreams . . . if you want to encourage the more peaceful kind and work with your dreams to understand their messages, sleep with howlite under your pillow. It helps you to access dream wisdom and allows you to remember it upon waking, so be sure to keep a dream diary by the side of your bed! An incredibly calming crystal, howlite is also powerful against insomnia, encouraging your waking mind to switch off, so that you can drift into a deep, dreamy sleep.

Celestite

Another crystal for dream work – especially for connecting to higher wisdom to gain answers through your dreams – is celestite. It will help your sleep and dreams to be calm and peaceful and is particularly powerful for those who struggle to sleep through the night without waking up. Keep celestite by your bedside to bring tranquillity and peace to your bedroom, so that you sleep soundly through the night.

Other crystals for sleeping soundly: moonstone, lepidolite, rose quartz or chrysoprase.

Note: do be mindful of how many crystals you have in your bedroom. If you are energy-sensitive, you might find that they stimulate your energy, keeping you awake. So try to keep only soothing, calming crystals (any of those mentioned in this chapter) in your bedroom if you do have trouble sleeping.

◆ Staying Wide Awake ◆

For those who find getting up and out of bed in the morning difficult and are constantly hitting the snooze button, try waking up to the crystals below. You can also try taking a few long, slow, deep breaths holding them for an energy boost during the day, rather than reaching for the caffeine when the 3pm slump hits.

Clear quartz

If you struggle to wake up and get going in the morning, try holding a piece of clear quartz for a few minutes first thing, perhaps visualising it filling you with energy, to give you a hit to start your day. This powerhouse of a crystal will raise and amplify your energies, setting you up for the day.

Sunstone and citrine

Try meditating with sunstone or citrine in the morning or carry them with you throughout the day to invite in some uplifting energy, light and life.

Carnelian

Carnelian will boost your energy levels and give you a spring in your step for the day ahead. Again, you can meditate with this in the morning or carry it with you as you go about your day.

Other crystals for staying wide awake: pyrite, tiger's eye, obsidian or bloodstone.

CHAPTER 15:

Crystals for . . .
Connecting to a Higher Power

Whether you want to connect to your own source of inner wisdom and guidance (or those of the universe, guides or angels), hear the voice of your intuition, live a more purposeful life or go into deeper states of meditation, crystals can help connect you to a source of higher power.

Many of the crystals mentioned in this section are high-vibration ones that will work on all the areas mentioned, all of which blend with one another: as you meditate daily, you will naturally connect more to your intuition; as you connect to and follow your intuition, you will naturally uncover your purpose; as you begin to live more on purpose, you will naturally connect to higher wisdom, and so on.

◆ Meditate, Meditate, Meditate ◆

One of the first and most important ways to connect to any kind of higher wisdom or power is through meditation. Meditation will help you to cut through the noise in your head, get beneath the turmoil of your emotions and quieten your world, so that you can hear, connect to and access deeper states of intuition, wisdom, guidance and knowledge.

Clear quartz

My first recommendation for deepening your meditation practice is clear quartz. This master crystal brings clarity to your mind to heal and raise your energies and vibrations, so that you can become more aligned with higher states of energy. Hold a clear quartz in your receiving hand as you meditate daily to deepen your practice and expand your awareness.

Selenite harmonisers

If you are only just starting out with meditation or struggle to clear your mind or find a state of calm in your practice, get a pair of selenite harmonisers (sometimes called rods). These are cylindrical pieces of selenite, and you hold one in each hand as you meditate to clear your mind and your energy field, so that you feel grounded, peaceful, balanced and calm during your practice.

Other crystals to help deepen your meditation practice: apatite, chrysoprase, smoky quartz or rose quartz.

◆ Listen to Your Intuition ◆

If you want to find a deeper connection to your intuition – that deeper wisdom within you that can nudge you along your life path – crystals are here to help.

Crystals for your third-eye and sacral chakras

Meditating with crystals over your third eye – the main portal to your intuition – will help to awaken your innate awareness. Kyanite is one of the most powerful crystals to begin with as it can gently stimulate and open your third eye, strengthening your intuition and inner wisdom.

I often hold a crystal over my third eye when I need answers and guidance, tapping into the wisdom within me. I will allow a situation or question to run through my mind's eye, as the power of the crystal helps me to access my intuitive answers. You may not hear the answer straight away, but trust that the part of you that needs to know knows, and the answers will become clear.

It's also vital to work with your sacral chakra when you want to tap more deeply into your intuition. Think of some of the things we say, such as 'I felt it in my

147

gut' – this describes intuitive guidance and it can very often get lost beneath the myriad emotions that we don't address, listen to or heal. Take a look at 'Soothing the Emotions' (p. 79) or 'Letting Go' (p. 121) for insight on how to heal your emotions, so you can begin to feel your intuition more.

You can harness the intuitive power of both your third-eye and sacral chakras by holding an associated crystal to meditate or by placing the crystals on the relevant chakra. Close your eyes and take deep breaths and imagine a link between your third-eye and sacral chakras, opening up an energetic line of intuition and wisdom that you can begin to tap into. You may imagine the energy moving one way with your inhale and the other way with your exhale. Work with your intuition daily and follow it as often as possible to strengthen it and build trust in yourself.

Other crystals for listening to your intuition: for your third eye: amethyst, moonstone, labradorite or sodalite; **and for your sacral chakra:** citrine, moonstone, sunstone or clear quartz.

◆ Finding Your Purpose ◆

If you're looking to find more purpose and meaning in life, meditate daily with the crystals below or wear them at all times to guide you along your way.

Sugilite

Sugilite is one of the best crystals for finding answers to all the big questions of life, such as who am I and why am I here? A deeply spiritual crystal, sugilite will help you to appreciate who you are and what you have to offer, remind you of your soul purpose and inspire you to live from love and follow it.

Selenite

Another powerful one for connecting with your soul and learning from your life experiences and how they lead you along your path of discovery, this high-vibration crystal will help you to hear and follow messages from the universe that guide you towards your soul's intent and purpose.

Charoite

Charoite will teach you about you and show you your part to play in the world. It will inspire you to be of service, awakening your soul gifts that only you can offer and encouraging you to share these gifts with the world so that everyone can benefit from your magic.

Howlite

Once you have found your purpose in life (and remember this can change over time), howlite will encourage you to remain on your path, committed to the journey ahead. It is also useful at the beginning of your journey. If ever you feel completely lost and directionless, howlite will work with you to find your way.

Other crystals for finding your purpose: clear quartz, labradorite, moldavite or amethyst.

◆ Connection to Higher Wisdom ◆ and Guidance

Whether you call it your higher self, the universe, source or soul, if you are looking for a connection to a higher source of wisdom and guidance, crystals can help to facilitate that, and your crown chakra is where you want to focus for this. Meditate lying down with a crystal above your crown or, if – like me – you much prefer sitting to meditate, hold your chosen crystal and visualise your crown chakra opening to guidance as you meditate.

Lapis lazuli

This stone of communication will not only help you connect to your higher self, but also to differentiate between the voice of your ego and that of your higher self and to be able to listen to and hear the latter more clearly. Meditate with or wear this crystal to stay connected to the wiser, all-knowing, higher part of you.

Blue goldstone

Although man-made, blue goldstone is a powerful crystal for divine connection; you can almost feel your connection to the whole universe just by looking at it. This crystal will help you to understand that everything is made up of energy and vibration and that you are part of the whole.

Celestite

Often associated with divine power, celestite brings higher spiritual awareness and connection to universal energies.

Labradorite

Labradorite is a magical crystal that helps you to communicate with higher guidance, connect to universal energies and explore past lives and the akashic records (vibrational records of all that ever has, is or will happen;

they hold a soul's journey and all the thoughts, feelings and deeds from each lifetime).

Apophyllite

Apophyllite will help to connect you to the spiritual realms and create a conscious connection between the spiritual and the physical.

Moldavite

One of my favourite crystals for receiving messages and guidance from higher realms is moldavite – but please use with caution, as it is incredibly powerful. Created when a meteorite crashed to earth approximately 15 million years ago, moldavite is not of this world and, as such, is said to have been sent here to help with the future of the earth.

Other crystals for connecting to higher wisdom and guidance: selenite, clear quartz or amethyst.

◆ Connecting to Guides and Angels ◆

For those of you with a belief and interest in spirit guides or angelic realms, crystals can help raise your vibration to access these celestial beings.

Try meditating with one of these crystals while being

open to hearing and receiving messages, guidance or signs. Then perhaps open your eyes and immediately begin journaling, seeing what messages flow. Or wear these crystals to remember that you are never alone and that angelic assistance is always nearby; touch your crystal and call on your guides in times of need.

Angelite

As its name suggests, angelite is all about connecting to guardian angels, knowing that they are close and feeling their support. One of my favourite crystals, you maybe remember me mentioning it in a story earlier (see p. 47).

Lapis lazuli

Lapis lazuli will help you connect to and communicate with your spirit guides, receiving their wisdom and guidance.

Danburite

This will help you to access higher levels of consciousness and your own inner guidance, also opening you up to receiving messages and signs from spirit guides and angels.

Petalite

Sometimes known as the angel stone, petalite helps to expand your levels of awareness to connect to your guardian angels.

Other crystals for connecting to guides and angels: selenite, apophyllite, celestite or kyanite.

CHAPTER 16:

Crystals for . . . the Zodiac Signs

Each sign of the zodiac carries different energies, qualities and traits and is associated with different crystals. These associations originate from many different sources, including the month you were born, which was later picked up by astrologers and linked to the zodiac signs, the ruling planet or element of each zodiac sign and how the energies of a particular crystal complement or counteract those of that sign.

Through the year, the sun moves through each sign of the zodiac, staying in each one for around a month, which is known as a season. No matter what our sun sign is (determined by which sign the sun was in at the time we were born), we are all influenced by and can work with the energies and qualities of each particular zodiac season as the sun makes its journey through them all.

Below I have listed some of the best crystals to use

for each sign of the zodiac. You may want to work with these crystals during that particular zodiac season (dates for these are given below) or when the moon is new or full in each zodiac sign (see Chapter 13, 'Crystals for . . . Moon Magic'). You may also want to choose a crystal to work with based on your sun, moon or rising sign, or have a look through some of the qualities that each sign and crystal offer and work with these crystals to invite a little more of this energy into your life.

ARIES
(21 March–19 April)

As the fiery first sign of the zodiac, Aries brings drive, ambition and motivation to get things started.

Carnelian
As a high-energy crystal that encourages creativity, carnelian brings a confidence boost to take the first step towards manifesting dreams and desires.

Bloodstone

Bloodstone helps you to take action in the present moment, which is useful, as Aries can have a tendency to rush off into hundreds of ideas and never complete any of them.

Aquamarine

If you are finding the Aries fire a little too much, this crystal will calm the flames, helping to clear the mind and soothe the emotions.

TAURUS

(20 April–20 May)

Taurus offers grounding, stability and security, bringing things down to earth. It is a sign associated with pleasure and encourages slowing down and self-care.

Rose quartz

Perfect for those self-worth, self-love and self-care vibes, rose quartz will help you to look after yourself and put your needs first.

Black tourmaline

A healing, protecting crystal with strong, earthy energy, tourmaline helps you to ground and feel safe and secure.

Malachite

If you're finding the Taurus vibes slowing you down to a stop or that you're stuck in a stubborn stand-off, malachite will help to get things moving.

GEMINI

(21 May–20 June)

Gemini brings a quick, lively energy that is focused on communication, information and ideas. This sign of the zodiac loves change.

Danburite

A powerful crystal for accessing your own inner guidance and gaining information and wisdom from within, it also facilitates change, helping you to leave the past behind.

Blue lace agate

The perfect communication crystal, this will help you to express yourself and speak your truth, saying what you think and feel.

Chrysocolla

If your mind is brimming with ideas you can't make sense of or you're feeling anxiety or fear of change, chrysocolla will bring order, calm and tranquillity.

CANCER

(21 June–22 July)

Deep, sensitive, nurturing and caring, Cancer is all about the emotions, which can ebb and flow just like the tides.

Rhodonite

A heart-opening crystal, rhodonite has a deeply healing energy that promotes unconditional love, compassion, peace and forgiveness.

Chrysoprase

Chrysoprase brings a nurturing energy that provides a sense of safety and security in which to process emotions and a feeling of deep trust.

Moonstone

Cancer is ruled by the moon, so this is the perfect crystal to help you to allow your emotions to flow, soothing and calming them if they become too intense.

LEO

(23 July–22 August)

Big, bold and brave, Leo energy is childlike and playful, asking you to open your heart, express yourself and shine in life.

Sunstone

Leo is ruled by the sun and, as the name suggests, sunstone is like holding a little piece of sunshine, bringing a sense of joy and happiness and encouraging you to shine.

Tiger's eye

Awakening your creativity and unlocking your true potential, tiger's eye brings Leo-like qualities of courage, power and self-belief.

Larimar

If you find yourself on the verge of a temper tantrum if you don't get your own way, or in a self-sabotage/doubt spiral, this crystal will bring you peace, calm and healing.

VIRGO

(23 August–22 September)

One of the most healing signs of the zodiac, Virgo is practical, logical and hard-working, focused on the finer details and solving problems.

Citrine

The ideal crystal to have on hand when you need to organise your thoughts, analyse information and find solutions to problems.

Sugilite

Also known as the healer's stone, sugilite helps to access deeper wisdom, not only from the thinking mind, but also intuition and a sixth sense.

Howlite

If you find yourself stuck in the self-critical, perfectionist nature of Virgo, howlite will help to quieten the inner critic, bringing compassion and patience.

LIBRA

(23 September–22 October)

Peace, harmony and equilibrium in relationships and life are what Libra is searching for, alongside a sense of justice and fairness.

Jade

A true crystal of tranquillity, harmony and peace, jade is also a bringer of luck in love, helping all of your relationships to flourish.

Apophyllite

One of the most calming crystals around, apophyllite emits tranquil, peaceful vibes, connecting you to love, happiness and higher realms.

Lapis lazuli

For those times when you find yourself in that Libra tendency of being indecisive, lapis will help you to take back control of your life.

SCORPIO

(23 October–21 November)

The alchemist of the zodiac, Scorpio brings transformation, transmutation and a deep dive into the depths of our being to understand ourselves better.

Obsidian

Black obsidian is a powerful crystal that takes us into our shadows and subconscious realms to bring healing and clarity. Snowflake obsidian is gentler.

Labradorite

A magical crystal of transformation, labradorite shines light into hidden truths, bringing what needs to be seen, understood and transformed to the surface.

Amethyst

If you find yourself overwhelmed by deep emotions, especially sadness, anger, fear or grief, amethyst will help you to find a deep understanding of them and the ability to release them gently.

SAGITTARIUS

(22 November–21 December)

The optimistic adventurer of the zodiac, Sagittarius loves to expand horizons and explore all there is to know about the world and life.

Turquoise

Used as a traveller's amulet in many ancient civilisations, this is the perfect companion to protect you as you undertake adventures and explorations.

Azurite

Azurite helps you to find purpose and direction, explore new realities and ways of expanding consciousness. It also helps to reveal truths.

Smoky quartz

If you find yourself running at the first sign of trouble, trying to escape reality or taking on too much, smoky quartz will help to ground and anchor you.

CAPRICORN

(22 December–19 January)

The most ambitious, hard-working sign of the zodiac, Capricorn is focused on reaching goals and succeeding in life.

Garnet

A crystal of commitment, garnet brings the motivation to stay until the job is done, helping to overcome any setbacks and bringing passion to the project.

Amber

Not strictly a crystal but a fossilised resin, amber motivates you to get what you want – if you can see it and believe it, amber will help you to achieve it.

Aragonite

If you are pushing yourself too hard or taking on too much, aragonite will help you to know that you are doing your best and make sure your expectations are realistic.

AQUARIUS
(20 January–18 February)

Freedom-seeking and future-driven, Aquarius is innovative, ingenious and humanitarian-focused, seeking authenticity and liberation.

Angelite

A 'new-age' crystal, known to raise conscious awareness, heighten perception and connect to higher realms, angelite helps you to know and speak your truth.

Apatite

Promoting humanitarian service, apatite shows how you can contribute to the collective good by being and expressing yourself. It will help you to seek freedom, always looking to the future and what's next.

Rhodochrosite

Aquarius can have a tendency to avoid emotions, shutting down and giving the cold shoulder. Rhodochrosite will help keep the heart open and process emotions.

PISCES

(19 February–20 March)

The final sign of the zodiac, Pisces is dreamy, empathetic and highly intuitive, bringing the knowledge that we are all connected and the ability to vision a new reality.

Fluorite

Helping you to strengthen your intuition and connect you to higher spiritual energies, fluorite encourages you to see the bigger picture of your life.

Ametrine

Bridging the gap between the spiritual and physical worlds, ametrine shows you how to bring dreams to action by tuning into your higher awareness.

Hematite

Pisces can sometimes have issues with setting boundaries, taking on and feeling the worries of the whole world; hematite will help you to set energetic and emotional boundaries and keep you grounded.

Conclusion

Thank you so much for taking this crystal journey with me. I hope that you now feel confident in the many ways through which you can invite the magic of crystals into your daily life to help you to care for yourself and bring healing and transformation.

Dip in and out of this book as often as you need to, and enjoy the process of discovering new crystals, as well as new ways of using them along the way. But remember that this is your journey, and that you know best. My greatest wish is that through reading this book and working with crystals you will discover what works for you, as you learn to trust in yourself and your intuition. There is no greater act of self-care. This is a lifelong journey, and crystals will be there for you every step of the way.

I always love to hear from you, so please share your crystal stories, tagging me on Instagram: @kirsty_gallagher_

Enjoy the crystal magic. I can't wait to see where it will take you . . .

Acknowledgements

To my wonderful family: Sandra, Kylie, Kerry, Liam, Stephanie, Soraya, Jake, Chloe, Edward, Isaac and my late Grandpa Donald. I love you all and thank you for always loving and supporting me.

To Sam, for being the best friend a girl could ever ask for, and to my godson, Harley, for loving crystals as much as I do.

My editor, Holly Whitaker – thank you for being the best and for your continual support and encouragement; I love creating books with you! And to all the wonderful people at Yellow Kite who have supported me on this journey, thank you. I am so grateful to Myrto Kalavrezou and Caitriona Horne for your PR and marketing skills, Anne Newman for your editing magic and Jo Myler for creating yet another book cover of dreams.

If you are holding this book in your hands, thank you for allowing me to share the crystal magic with you. I hope it changes your life as much as it has mine.

Eternal gratitude to you if you bought my book *Lunar Living*, as you helped to make it a *Sunday Times* Bestseller, not just once, but three times! Thank you for all your support – you are the best community ever and I appreciate you more than you know.

My Lunar Living online sisterhood: thank you for all your support, lunar love and for being the best sisterhood ever. My never-ending gratitude to my right-hand woman, Helen Elias – nothing I do would be what it is without you.

To all of you who have attended my 'Soul Space' online lunar yoga and meditation workshops, 'Sacred Space' wheel of the year workshops and 'Still Space' meditations, along with all my IG followers; thank you for being a part of this magical community and continuing to show up for yourselves and each other. Remember, you are never alone – you've got this, I've got you, we've got each other.

So much love and gratitude to these special people in my life: Becki Rabin, Megan Rose Lane, Wendy O'Beirne, Caggie Dunlop, Emma Taylor, Hannah Holt, Lisa Strong, Rebecca Dennis, Ian Steed – my life would not be the same without you in it.

To my Soul Alignment and Aligned clients: you are the absolute dream to work with. Thank you for your willingness to trust me with your hearts and souls. I love seeing you show up and make such a huge difference in the world. I am so proud of you.

Thank you to everyone at ITV's *This Morning* (especially Holly and Phillip) and *The Chris Evans Breakfast Show* for all your support over the past year and for allowing me to share the moon magic with the nation. Thanks, too, to Fearne Cotton, Warehouse, *You*, *Red*, *Stylist* and *Happiful* magazines and everyone who has invited me on to their podcasts or let me share my work with their audiences.

If I have not named you, it's not because you are forgotten or that I am not grateful. It's simply that I have been blessed to have so many wonderful people touch my life and there are not enough pages to mention you all; it would be another book in itself! If you have ever been a part of my life in any way, thank you.

About the Author

Photograph by Jen Armstrong

Kirsty Gallagher is a moon mentor, soul-alignment and spiritual coach, yoga teacher, meditation teacher and *Sunday Times* bestselling author with an infectious passion for life.

She has been sharing the life-changing benefits of yoga and the moon for 13 years through classes, workshops and private and corporate sessions, and has taught over 80 worldwide retreats. She is author of the *Sunday Times* bestselling book *Lunar Living* and founder of the online sisterhood Lunar Living, which teaches how to weave the secret and ancient wisdom of the moon into modern, everyday life.

Kirsty has created a worldwide community through her Soul Space lunar yoga and meditation classes and her Sacred Space seasonal yoga, meditation and ritual classes. One of her greatest passions is bringing people together, showing us that we are never alone.

Kirsty works alongside women in one-to-one and group mentoring programmes, teaching them to live back in alignment with an ancient cycle, a natural rhythm and flow, so helping them to connect back into their inner wisdom, power, authenticity and purpose. Weaving lunar, nature and divine feminine wisdom with spiritual teachings, astrology and cutting-edge transformational coaching techniques, Kirsty helps women to overcome doubts, fears and self-sabotage to know and trust in themselves like never before and find greater meaning and purpose in life.

Kirsty is a sought-after leading voice in lunar wisdom and has shared moon magic on *The Chris Evans Breakfast Show* and *This Morning*. She has also been featured in *You*, *Stylist*, *Red*, *Women's Health*, *Soul & Spirit* and *Natural Health* magazines.

Described as down to earth, warm-hearted, compassionate and inspiring, Kirsty is known for bringing ancient mystical practices and wisdom to modern-day life in a relatable way that anyone and everyone can take something from. Find out more at kirstygallagher.com.

If you enjoyed reading *Crystals for Self-Care,*
why don't you read Kirsty's other books,
Lunar Living and *The Lunar Living Journal*?

books to help you live a good life

Join the conversation and tell
us how you live a #goodlife

🐦 @yellowkitebooks
📘 YellowKiteBooks
📌 Yellow Kite Books
📷 YellowKiteBooks